QUICK MEALS IN A WOK

CHARMAINE SOLOMON

HAMLYN

Published 1993 by Hamlyn Australia,
an imprint of the Octopus Publishing Group,
a division of Reed International Books Australia Pty Ltd
22 Salmon Street, Port Melbourne, Victoria 3207

Designed by Louise Lavarack
Photographs by Michael Cook
Styling by Margaret Alcock
Food cooked by Nina Harris, Jill Pavey
China: Villeroy & Boch, Australia Pty Ltd
Typeset in 9½ on 12 pt Berkeley Old Style Book by Midland Typesetters
Produced in Hong Kong by Mandarin Offset

National Library of Australia
   cataloguing-in-publication data:

Solomon, Charmaine.
   Quick meals in a wok.

   Includes index.
   ISBN 0 947334 47 5.

   1. Wok cookery. 2. Cookery, Oriental. I. Title. (Series: Asian
   cooking library).

641.589

Introduction

ALL ABOUT WOKS   The wok is, I would say, the most popular cooking utensil in the world . . . not only is it the mainstay of Chinese kitchens but, by one name or another, you will find it throughout Asia.

Western manufacturers also pay it the compliment of trying (not always successfully) to duplicate its good design. Usually, however, they are not quite deep enough and sometimes use unsuitable materials. Stainless steel, for instance, a notoriously bad conductor of heat, may make a good-looking wok but not a good cooking one. Non-stick linings may not stick but often burn.

The original wok is such a sensible utensil. It has no corners to catch and burn; the high sides make it easy to toss and stir food without having it end up all over the stove; and it requires very little oil when frying, because of its shape. It is ideal for stir-frying (a marvellously quick way of cooking—often taking less than 5 minutes actual cooking time) but remember to have all your ingredients ready—sliced, diced, chopped and measured, before you turn on the heat. Stir-frying is easy if you keep your mind on what you are doing and toss the ingredients in at the precise moment.

The wok can also be used for steaming, braising, simmering, stewing or frying. Steaming is traditionally done in a bamboo steamer, but you can improvise by putting a trivet in the wok on which to rest the dish containing food. Use a cover large enough to go over the food and make contact with the side of the wok so steam doesn't escape. Woks aren't usually sold complete with covers, but you'll find suitable covers in the same stores. A high domed cover is most versatile.

In Asia, woks are used mostly over fuel stoves, often just a clay bowl with fire in it. In western kitchens, gas is ideal for wok cooking but if your cooking area does not have gas laid on, it is possible to buy wok burners which use bottled LP gas. These are a worthwhile investment if you frequently stir-fry and are great for outdoor cooking too.

If all you have is an electric hotplate, buy a wok made in heavier metal with a flattened base so it makes better contact with the heat. And because electric hotplates take some time to heat up and cool down, you must cook on highest heat and lift the wok off the hotplate when the cooking is done.

Try working with two hotplates—one set to maximum and one on medium low. It involves a little to- and fro-ing but affords better control.

Electric woks are handsome, and preferable to using a wok on an electric hotplate, but the heat is slow to build up. Remember, for best results, cook only small amounts of food at a time.

CHOOSING A WOK   The most reasonably priced woks are rolled steel but they have the disadvantage of rusting if not used frequently and dried scrupulously after use. They also have to be seasoned before use. A rolled steel wok is usually coated with oil to prevent it rusting between factory and consumer. Sometimes this coating will come off with a good scrub in hot soapy water, but often it is stubborn and needs to be softened first. Do this by filling the wok with water, adding 2 or 3 tablespoons of bicarbonate of soda (baking soda) and boiling for 15 minutes. The coating can then be removed with a fine scourer. If necessary, repeat the process until there is no coating left on the inside. (Never mind the outside, it will burn off as you use the wok.)

The only other woks I recommend are enamel-coated woks. They never rust and will not impart a metallic flavour or greyish colour to any food left in them. If you use an ordinary steel wok, remember to remove food as soon as it is cooked.

SEASONING YOUR STEEL WOK   Dry the wok well and put it over gentle heat. When the metal is hot, wipe over the entire inner surface with a wad of absorbent kitchen paper dipped in peanut oil. Repeat a number of times, using fresh paper each time. At first the paper will come away a rusty brown, but after a few times it remains clean. The wok is then ready for use.

After cooking, do not scrub with steel wool or abrasives or you will have to do the seasoning all over again. Soak in hot water to soften any food which sticks, then rub gently with a sponge. Dry the wok well and, before putting it away, heat it to make sure it is quite dry; the tiniest amount of moisture will cause it to rust. The best insurance against rust, however, is to use your wok often. A well seasoned wok develops a shiny black cooking surface which is quite normal and makes it even better to cook in. If you don't use the wok frequently, rub over the cooking surface with paper dipped in oil before putting it away.

Some people prefer a wok with a single handle, but personally I find it heavy to lift with one hand and prefer the traditional two-handled wok. But do remember to grab a pot holder before you grab the metal handles.

SUCCESSFUL STIR-FRYING   As this book is about quick cooking, you will find I have particularly concentrated on stir frying. What is stir-frying? In western cooking, stirring implies a circular motion. If you have ever watched an Oriental cook at work, you know that the action is more like tossing, flipping, keeping food constantly on the move so that all of it comes in contact with the hot wok.

Because the cooking takes just a few minutes once started, it is important to have all the ingredients ready or the whole performance will be spoilt. There can be no rushing to find something which should be added during the split-second timing. Have meat and vegetables sliced, garlic crushed, ginger grated, sauces and stock measured and ready. Arrange everything on a tray within reach, preferably in the correct order for adding to the wok. Run through the recipe in your mind before heating the wok. There is no time for checking a recipe once the action starts!

Speed and convenience aside, there is another advantage. Stir-frying requires very little oil, resulting in delicious, healthy, easy to digest meals.

VEGETABLES

Be ready to eat immediately after cooking or the lettuce will lose its crispness and with it, most of its appeal. A good winter way to enjoy lettuce.

BRAISED LETTUCE
Braise, serves 2 to 4

- 1 large, firm head of iceberg lettuce
- 1 tablespoon peanut oil
- ½ teaspoon crushed garlic
- ½ teaspoon finely grated fresh ginger
- 2 tablespoons chicken stock
- 1 teaspoon sugar
- 2 teaspoons light soy sauce
- 1 teaspoon cornflour

Wash, drain and dry lettuce. Cut into quarters lengthwise, then cut quarters twice across. Heat oil in wok, add garlic, ginger and lettuce in quick succession, tossing for 1 minute. Push lettuce aside. Add stock, sugar, soy sauce, and cornflour blended with 1 tablespoon water. Quickly boil to thicken, mix lettuce through and serve on its own or accompanying a meal.

HONEY GLAZED MUSHROOMS
Stir-fry, serves 4

- *300 g (10 oz) button mushrooms*
- *1 tablespoon peanut oil*
- *1 tablespoon honey*
- *1 tablespoon soy sauce*
- *1 teaspoon oriental sesame oil*

Wipe mushrooms with damp paper towel and trim stalks. Heat oil in a wok, add mushrooms and stir-fry for 1 minute over medium heat. Stir in honey and soy sauce, lower heat and cover. Simmer for 3 minutes. Uncover and cook until liquid reduces and thickens, stirring to coat mushrooms in glaze. Turn off heat, sprinkle with sesame oil and mix. Serve hot or cold as an accompaniment to Chinese style dishes.

Dried wood fungus (also known as wood ear or black fungus) comes in small or large sizes. Here I have used the large variety, about 7 cm (3 in) across in dried form and swelling to many times that size when soaked. If you can find only the smaller variety (about 1 cm across), use ½ cup.

CLOUD EARS IN HOI SIN SAUCE
Stir-fry, serves 4

- 6–8 pieces dried wood fungus
- 2 teaspoons hoi sin sauce
- 2 tablespoons light soy sauce
- 2 teaspoons peanut oil
- ½ teaspoon crushed garlic
- 2 cups gai larn in bite-size pieces
- 1 teaspoon cornflour
- 1 teaspoon oriental sesame oil

Rinse wood fungus. Place in large bowl and cover generously with hot water. Soak 10 minutes. Fungus will more than double in size. Drain and cut into bite-size pieces, discarding tough, gritty parts. Mix hoi sin and soy sauces with ¼ cup water. Heat peanut oil and fry garlic and gai larn for a few seconds, add sauce mixture and wood fungus and stir until mixture boils. Mix cornflour with 2 tablespoons cold water, add to wok and cook until liquid thickens. Stir in sesame oil and serve immediately with rice or noodles.

3

CORN AND SUGAR SNAP PEAS
Stir-fry, serves 4

- 1 x 440 g (15 oz) can young corn cobs or fresh baby corn
- 250 g (8 oz) sugar snap peas or snow peas
- 1 tablespoon peanut oil
- 1 small clove garlic, crushed
- ½ teaspoon finely grated fresh ginger
- 1 tablespoon oyster sauce
- 1 teaspoon sugar
- 1 teaspoon oriental sesame oil

Remove husks and silk from fresh corn, or drain canned corn. Top, tail and string peas. Heat peanut oil in wok, fry garlic and ginger for 10 seconds, add corn and peas and stir-fry 1 minute on high heat. Add oyster sauce, sugar and 2 tablespoons water and cook 1 minute longer. Stir in sesame oil, serve immediately.

INDONESIAN STIR-FRIED VEGETABLES
Stir-fry, serves 4

- 4 cups prepared vegetables of choice (cabbage, beans, celery, spring onions, etc.)
- 2 tablespoons vegetable oil
- 2 cloves garlic, crushed
- 2 onions, finely chopped
- sprig fresh curry leaves or 10 dried curry leaves
- ½ teaspoon dried shrimp paste
- 1 tablespoon ketjap manis (sweetened dark soy)

Wash vegetables and drain well. In a wok, heat oil and fry garlic, onion, curry leaves and shrimp paste over medium heat, crushing shrimp paste with back of cooking spoon. Cook, stirring frequently, until onion is transparent. Add vegetables, those which require longer cooking in first, and stir-fry until tender but still crisp. Add ketjap manis to taste.

CHINESE STIR-FRIED VEGETABLES
Stir-fry, serves 6

- 1 cup cauliflower florets
- 1 cup broccoli florets
- 2 carrots, thinly sliced
- 125 g (4 oz) snow peas or sugar snap peas
- 1 red capsicum
- 250 g (8 oz) mushrooms
- 2 tablespoons peanut oil
- 2 cloves garlic, crushed
- 1 teaspoon finely grated fresh ginger
- 2 tablespoons light soy sauce
- ½ cup vegetable stock
- 2 teaspoons cornflour

Blanch cauliflower, broccoli and carrot until tender but still crunchy. Reserve cooking liquid for vegetable stock. Wash and string peas and cut capsicum into thin strips. Trim stems off mushrooms, cutting caps into thick slices.

Heat oil in wok and stir-fry garlic and ginger for 30 seconds. Add peas, capsicum and mushrooms and stir-fry on high heat for 1 minute. Stir in soy sauce and vegetable stock. Add cornflour mixed with 2 tablespoons cold water and stir until liquid clears and thickens. Toss in blanched vegetables and heat through. Serve immediately with steamed rice.

A robust dish. Serve cold as an hors d'oeuvre or hot with rice.

SZECHWAN-STYLE EGGPLANT
Deep-fry, serves 6 to 8

- 1 kg (2 lb) eggplants
- 2 cups peanut oil
- 2 teaspoons finely grated ginger
- 2 teaspoons finely chopped garlic
- 1 red capsicum, cut in large squares
- 6 spring onions, sliced diagonally

SAUCE
- ½ cup dark soy sauce
- ¼ cup Chinese black vinegar or cider vinegar
- 1 tablespoon dry sherry
- 1 tablespoon sugar
- 2 teaspoons oriental sesame oil
- 2 teaspoons sweet chilli sauce

Wash and dry eggplants. Do not peel. Cut into large cubes and fry small amounts in hot oil till golden brown, removing with a slotted spoon. Pour off oil, leaving 1 tablespoon.

Mix ingredients for sauce, stirring to dissolve sugar. Reheat oil and fry ginger, garlic, capsicum and spring onions on low heat until garlic is golden. Add sauce and boil. Add eggplant and toss until most of the sauce is absorbed.

A high-protein vegetarian main dish to serve with rice or on its own.

BEAN CURD WITH PEANUTS
Deep-fry, serves 4

- 500 g (1 lb) firm bean curd
- peanut oil for frying
- ⅓ cup raw peanuts
- 1 teaspoon crushed garlic
- ½ teaspoon dried shrimp paste
- ½ cup crunchy peanut butter
- 2 tablespoons ketjap manis (sweetened dark soy)
- ½ teaspoon sambal ulek
- 1 teaspoon palm sugar or brown sugar
- 3 tablespoons vinegar
- ⅓ cup canned coconut milk
- 1 cup shredded cabbage
- 1 cup fresh bean sprouts
- 3 spring onions, finely sliced

Place bean curd between paper towels, pressing gently to dry. This will minimise spattering when frying. Cut into small dice. In hot oil, fry bean curd until golden. Lift out and drain on paper towels. Fry peanuts for 3 to 4 minutes; lift out on slotted spoon and drain on paper until cool enough to rub off skins.

Pour off all but 1 tablespoon of oil and fry garlic and shrimp paste over low heat, stirring and mashing with back of spoon. Add peanut butter, ketjap manis, sambal ulek, sugar and vinegar. Remove from heat. Gradually stir in coconut milk until sauce is of a thick pouring consistency.

Place bean curd on serving dish and spoon sauce over. Scatter cabbage and bean sprouts over and garnish with spring onions and fried peanuts.

Use your imagination and substitute other vegetables. Look for contrasting colours and textures.

MIXED BRAISED VEGETABLES
Braise, serves 4

- 2 tablespoons peanut oil
- 1 teaspoon finely chopped garlic
- 1 teaspoon finely chopped fresh ginger
- 1 cup sliced celery
- 1 cup sliced red and green capsicums
- 1 cup sliced Chinese broccoli
- ½ cup sliced spring onions
- 1 tablespoon light soy sauce
- 1 tablespoon oyster sauce
- 2 teaspoons cornflour

Heat oil in wok and, over low heat, cook garlic and ginger for 1 minute without browning. Add vegetables and stir-fry for 2 minutes on high heat. Add soy and oyster sauces mixed with ½ cup water. Cover and cook for 2 to 3 minutes on low heat. Mix cornflour with 1 tablespoon cold water and stir into liquid until it boils and thickens. Serve with hot steamed rice.

Fried Bean Curd with Pungent Sauce
Deep-fry, serves 6

- 500 g (1 lb) firm bean curd
- peanut oil for frying
- 250 g (8 oz) fresh bean sprouts, washed and drained
- 1/3 cup ketjap manis or dark soy sauce
- 1 tablespoon palm sugar or brown sugar
- 1 onion, roughly chopped
- 1 teaspoon sambal ulek
- 1 clove garlic
- 6 spring onions, finely sliced

Drain bean curd on paper towels and cut into dice. Deep-fry in hot oil until brown and drain. Place on a bed of bean sprouts. Put soy sauce, sugar, onion, sambal ulek and garlic in a blender container and blend until smooth. Spoon over bean curd and garnish with spring onions.

Stir-fried Beans and Zucchini
Stir-fry, serves 4

- 300 g (10 oz) long (snake) beans or french beans
- 1 large zucchini
- 2 tablespoons oil
- 1 teaspoon black mustard seeds
- 1 teaspoon ground turmeric
- 1 clove garlic, finely chopped
- salt to taste
- sprig of fresh curry leaves or 10 dried curry leaves

Trim ends off beans and cut into bite-size lengths. Cut zucchini into similar sized strips. Heat oil in wok and fry mustard seeds until they pop. Reduce heat and add turmeric, garlic, salt and curry leaves. Add beans and stir-fry for 1 minute over medium heat. Add 1/2 cup of water, cover and simmer for 5 minutes or until just tender. Add zucchini and stir-fry until almost all liquid has evaporated. Serve with rice.

I love the colours of brilliant green asparagus and bright red capsicums in this quick and delicious dish.

STIR-FRIED ASPARAGUS AND CAPSICUM, THAI STYLE
Stir-fry, serves 6 to 8

- 500 g (1 lb) asparagus
- 2 red capsicums
- 2 teaspoons finely chopped garlic
- 2 teaspoons green peppercorns, fresh or brined
- 2 tablespoons fish sauce
- 2 tablespoons Maggi Seasoning
- 1 tablespoon sugar
- 2 red chillies, sliced (optional)
- 3 tablespoons peanut oil

Wash vegetables and dry on paper towels. Snap off tough ends of asparagus and cut spears into bite-size lengths. Cut capsicum into strips of similar size. Combine garlic, crushed peppercorns, sauces, sugar and chilli. Stir until sugar dissolves.

Heat oil in wok and stir-fry vegetables on high heat until colours intensify. Add ¼ cup water, cover and steam for 2 to 3 minutes until vegetables are tender but still crisp. Add combined seasonings, stir until sauce boils and serve immediately with rice.

HEAVENLY BRAISED VEGETABLES
Braise, serves 4

- *10 dried shiitake (Chinese) mushrooms*
- *4 large pieces dried wood fungus*
- *1 cup sliced winter bamboo shoot*
- *1 x 440 g (15 oz) can young corn cobs or fresh baby corn*
- *1 tablespoon peanut oil*
- *1 tablespoon oriental sesame oil*
- *1 tablespoon soy sauce*
- *1 tablespoon oyster sauce*
- *1 tablespoon sugar*

Soak mushrooms in hot water to cover for 30 minutes. Discard stems, squeeze moisture from caps and cut in halves, quarters if large. Reserve soaking liquid. Soak wood fungus in fresh cold water for 20 minutes. Drain and cut into bite-size pieces. Discard gritty bits.

Heat oils in wok and brown mushrooms. Add 2 cups reserved mushroom liquid and remaining ingredients, except for wood fungus. Reduce heat and simmer, covered, for 25 minutes or until mushrooms are tender and liquid is reduced and syrupy. Add wood fungus and simmer 5 minutes longer. Serve with rice.

VEGETABLES, INDONESIAN STYLE
Simmer, serves 6

- *750 g (1½ lb) mixed seasonal vegetables (cauliflower, broccoli, beans, cabbage, zucchini, pumpkin, etc.)*
  - *2 tablespoons peanut oil*
  - *2 onions, finely chopped*
  - *2 teaspoons crushed garlic*
  - *1 teaspoon chopped red chilli or sambal ulek*
  - *1 teaspoon dried shrimp paste*
- *1 stalk lemon grass or 2 strips lemon rind, finely chopped*
  - *1 large ripe tomato, peeled, seeded and chopped*
    - *2 cups chicken stock*
    - *1 cup canned coconut milk*
    - *1 tablespoon peanut butter*
  - *2 teaspoons ketjap manis (sweetened dark soy)*
    - *lemon juice, optional*

Cut vegetables into small pieces; cauliflower or broccoli in sprigs, beans sliced diagonally, cabbage roughly shredded then cut crosswise, zucchini and pumpkin sliced or diced.

Heat oil in wok and stir-fry onion until soft and golden. Add garlic, chilli and shrimp paste and fry on low heat for 2 minutes, crushing shrimp paste with back of spoon. Add lemon grass or rind and tomato. Cook, stirring, until reduced. Add stock and coconut milk and bring to simmer, uncovered. (If coconut milk is very thick, add 1 cup water.) Add vegetables, putting those which require longer cooking in first, and toss until tender but still crisp. Stir in peanut butter and ketjap manis. Add a squeeze of lemon juice for extra tang.

So you thought bean curd was bland? Try this dish and think again.

Tofu in Hot Sauce
Simmer, serves 4

- 500 g (1 lb) fresh soft bean curd
- 1 tablespoon peanut oil
- 1 teaspoon finely chopped ginger
- 1 clove garlic, finely chopped
- 3 spring onions, sliced diagonally
- 1 teaspoon chilli bean paste
- 1 tablespoon tomato sauce
- salt to taste
- 1 teaspoon sugar
- 1 teaspoon dark soy sauce
- 2 teaspoons cornflour

Cut bean curd into 1 cm (½ in) cubes. Bring 4 cups water to boil in wok, add bean curd and simmer gently until heated through. Remove with strainer and leave to drain.

Dry wok, heat oil and stir-fry ginger and garlic until fragrant. Add ½ cup water and remaining ingredients, except spring onions and cornflour, and bring to boil. Blend cornflour with 1 tablespoon water, stir into sauce and cook, stirring, for a couple of minutes until clear and thick. Add spring onions and warm bean curd to sauce and toss gently to coat. Serve immediately with steamed rice.

PINEAPPLE COCONUT CURRY
Simmer, serves 6

- 1 slightly under-ripe pineapple
- 1 tablespoon peanut oil
- 1 onion, finely chopped
- 2 cloves garlic, finely chopped
- 1 fresh red chilli, seeded and sliced
- small stick cinnamon
- 2 whole cloves
- 3 cardamom pods, bruised
- 1 tablespoon ground coriander
- 2 teaspoons ground cummin
- salt to taste
- 1 cup canned coconut milk
- 1 teaspoon palm sugar or brown sugar
- ¼ cup dried shrimp
- 2 tablespoons fried shallots or onion flakes
- 2 teaspoons granulated sugar
- ½ teaspoon chilli powder

Peel pineapple and, with a series of diagonal cuts, remove rows of 'eyes'. Quarter lengthwise and trim away core. Cut pineapple into thick slices. Heat oil in wok and fry onion, garlic, chilli and whole spices over medium heat, stirring frequently, until onion is transparent. Add ground spices and salt and cook, stirring, until spices brown. Add pineapple and toss until coated with spice mixture. Add coconut milk and palm sugar and bring to simmer, stirring constantly. Simmer, uncovered, for 3 to 4 minutes, or until pineapple is just tender. Remove from heat. Pulverise shrimp in blender, combine with granulated sugar, fried shallots and chilli powder. Sprinkle over curry and serve with rice.

BEAN CURD WITH PEAS
Simmer, serves 4

- 2 tablespoons peanut oil
- 500 g (1 lb) fresh soft bean curd, drained
- 3 cloves garlic
- salt to taste
- ½ teaspoon finely grated fresh ginger
- 1 tablespoon light soy sauce
- 2 teaspoons honey
- 1 tablespoon dry sherry
- ½ teaspoon five spice powder
- ½ cup chicken stock
- 1 cup cooked peas
- ⅓ cup chopped spring onions
- 2 teaspoons cornflour

Blot moisture from bean curd by pressing between a double thickness of kitchen paper. Heat oil in wok and fry bean curd on low heat a few minutes, turning once. Crush garlic with salt and mix with ginger, soy sauce, honey, sherry, five spice powder and stock. Add to wok and simmer for 3 minutes. Blend cornflour with 1 tablespoon cold water and add to wok. Stir gently and bring to boil. When sauce thickens, add peas and spring onions and heat through. Serve with rice or noodles.

Eggplant is especially delicious when fried, but how it does soak up oil! Try steaming or boiling instead, adding spiciness with this sauce.

STEAMED EGGPLANT WITH SPICY SAUCE
Serves 6

- *750 g (1½ lb) firm eggplants*
- *2 tablespoons peanut oil*
- *1 teaspoon dried shrimp paste*
- *5 brazil nuts, finely grated*
- *1 teaspoon finely chopped galangal in brine or laos powder*
- *1 fresh red chilli, finely chopped*
- *2 tablespoons dark soy sauce*
- *2 teaspoons palm sugar or brown sugar*
- *½ cup canned coconut milk*
- *1 tablespoon tamarind extract*

Peel eggplant and dice. Place in a steamer and steam over boiling water until tender. Drain. Heat wok, add oil and fry shrimp paste over low heat, stirring constantly and mashing with back of cooking spoon. Add grated nuts and fry, stirring, for 1 minute. Add galangal, chilli, soy sauce, sugar, coconut milk and tamarind extract dissolved in ¼ cup hot water. Stir and simmer gently until heated through. Pour over eggplant and serve with rice.

SEAFOOD

Whichever method of cooking you employ, the secret with seafood is not to overcook it.

STIR-FRIED PRAWNS WITH OYSTER SAUCE
Stir-fry, serves 4

- *750 g (1½ lb) raw prawns*
- *3 stalks celery*
- *1 small red capsicum*
- *2 tablespoons peanut oil*
- *2 cloves garlic, crushed*
- *1 teaspoon finely grated fresh ginger*
- *2 tablespoons oyster sauce*
- *2 tablespoons dry sherry*
- *2½ teaspoons cornflour*

Shell and devein prawns. Cut celery in thin diagonal slices and capsicum into pieces of similar size. Heat oil and stir-fry garlic and ginger over low heat until soft and golden. Increase heat to medium, add prawns and stir-fry just until colour changes. Add vegetables and toss 1 minute more. Add oyster sauce, sherry, ½ cup water and bring to boil. Mix cornflour with 2 tablespoons cold water and pour into wok. Cook, stirring, until liquid thickens and becomes clear. Serve at once with hot rice.

STIR-FRIED PRAWNS WITH LYCHEES
Stir-fry, serves 4 to 6

- *750 g (1½ lb) medium-size raw prawns*
  - *1 teaspoon cornflour*
    - *½ teaspoon salt*
  - *1 tablespoon egg white*
- *½ teaspoon finely grated ginger*
    - *1 red capsicum*
  - *24 fresh or canned lychees*
  - *2 tablespoons peanut oil*

SAUCE
  - *2 teaspoons tomato paste*
- *2 tablespoons rice vinegar or white wine vinegar*
    - *1 teaspoon cornflour*
      - *1 teaspoon sugar*
        - *salt to taste*

Shell prawns, leaving tail on. Remove vein and slit prawns
almost through on back curve. Rinse in cold water and dry
on paper towels. Mix prawns with cornflour, salt, egg white
and ginger, cover and chill 30 minutes. Cut capsicum into
squares, discarding seeds and membrane. Peel and seed fresh
lychees or, if canned, drain well. Combine sauce ingredients
with ¼ cup water, stirring until sugar dissolves.

Heat 1 tablespoon oil in wok and stir-fry prawns, tossing

until they turn pink and start to curl. Remove from wok. Wash out wok, add remaining oil and stir-fry capsicum for 1 minute. Return prawns to wok, add lychees and sauce, stirring constantly, until sauce thickens. Serve immediately with hot rice.

PRAWNS WITH BLACK BEANS
Stir-fry, serves 4

- *750 g (1½ lb) large raw prawns*
- *3 cloves garlic, crushed*
- *1 teaspoon finely grated fresh ginger*
- *1 tablespoon dry sherry*
- *salt to taste*
- *1 red capsicum*
- *1 green capsicum*
- *2 tablespoons canned salted black beans*
- *1 tablespoon hot or sweet chilli sauce (optional)*
- *1 tablespoon soy sauce*
- *2 tablespoons peanut oil*
- *spring onion curls (see Note)*

Shell prawns, slit back and remove sandy tract. Rinse and blot dry on paper towels. Mix with garlic, ginger, sherry and salt and leave to marinate. Cut capsicums in diamond shapes. Rinse black beans and drain, mash with a fork and mix with chilli and soy sauces.

Heat wok and add oil, stir-fry capsicums for 2 minutes. Push to side of wok and cook prawns, stir-frying over high heat until they turn pink—about 2 minutes. Move prawns to one side of wok and add a little more oil. Stir in black bean mixture and cook, stirring, for 30 seconds. Mix prawns and capsicums into sauce and toss until coated with black bean mixture. Garnish with spring onion curls and serve at once.

Note To make spring onion curls, slit green portion several times with a pin and drop into iced water for 5 to 10 minutes.

With the price of scallops these days, extending this dish with vegetables is not only delicious, but also sensible.

STIR-FRIED SCALLOPS WITH SNOW PEAS
Stir-fry, serves 2 to 3

- 250 g (8 oz) scallops
- 4 spring onions
- 125 g (4 oz) snow peas or sugar snap peas
- 2 tablespoons peanut oil
- 1 teaspoon finely grated fresh ginger
- 1 clove garlic, finely chopped
- 2 teaspoons cornflour
- 2 teaspoons light soy sauce
- salt and sugar
- ½ teaspoon oriental sesame oil

Clean scallops and dry on kitchen paper. Cut spring onions, white and green parts, into bite-size pieces. String snow peas.

Heat peanut oil in wok and stir-fry peas for 1 minute. Add spring onions, ginger and garlic, stir-fry 15 seconds. Remove to a plate. Mix cornflour with soy sauce and ½ cup water. Pour into wok and cook, stirring, until thickened, about 1 minute. Add scallops and simmer for 1 minute, just until they begin to turn opaque. Stir in vegetables. Season to taste with salt and a pinch of sugar, stir in sesame oil and serve immediately with hot rice.

Many years ago I created this dish and, to my surprise, was served it at a special lunch in Hong Kong recently. In a banquet of many courses, one or two large prawns per serving are ample, but if served with only one other dish and rice, it will yield fewer portions.

CRYSTAL PRAWNS WITH GREEN VEGETABLE
Serves 4 to 8

- *16 large raw prawns*
- *salt*
- *1 egg white, beaten slightly*
- *3 teaspoons cornflour*
- *1 head firm, fresh broccoli or 1 bundle tender asparagus*
- *1 tablespoon peanut oil*
- *½ teaspoon finely grated fresh ginger*
- *1 small clove garlic, crushed*
- *1 tablespoon dry sherry*
- *2 teaspoons cornflour*
- *2 tablespoons shredded red ginger in syrup*
- *green part of 1 spring onion, finely sliced*

Shell and devein prawns, leaving tail on. In a bowl, sprinkle prawns with 1 teaspoon salt and stir vigorously with a wooden spoon or with chopsticks, for 1 full minute. Rinse in a colander under cold running water for 1 minute. Repeat twice more, using a teaspoon of salt each time and beating prawns well. (This ensures a crisp texture when cooked.) After final rinsing, dry on kitchen towels. With point of a sharp knife make a small slit through underside of prawns. Return to bowl and add egg white, ½ teaspoon salt and 3 teaspoons cornflour. Mix to thoroughly coat prawns. Cover and chill for 1 hour.

Cut broccoli into florets, leaving about 5 cm (2 in) of green stem on each piece. Push end of stem through slit in prawn so that floret rests within curve. If using asparagus, snap off tough ends and pass spear through prawn. Reserve any extra vegetable. Half fill a wok with water and when boiling, drop in prawns and vegetable. Stir. As soon as prawns become pink and vegetable a brilliant green, drain in colander.

Dry wok, add oil and fry fresh ginger and garlic for a few seconds. Add dry sherry and ⅓ cup water. Add cornflour mixed with 1 tablespoon cold water to wok and stir until sauce thickens. Drop prawns and vegetables in and toss lightly to coat. Serve at once, garnished with shredded red ginger and spring onion slices. Accompany with hot white rice.

PRAWNS IN COCONUT MILK
Simmer, serves 6

- *1 kg (2 lb) medium-size raw prawns*
- *1 cup canned coconut milk*
- *2 cloves garlic, finely chopped*
- *1 tablespoon finely chopped fresh ginger*
- *2 tablespoons fish sauce*
- *1 teaspoon sugar*
- *¼ teaspoon ground black pepper*
- *2 tablespoons fresh lime juice*

Shell and devein prawns. Put coconut milk, ½ cup water, garlic, ginger, fish sauce, sugar and pepper into wok and bring to boil while stirring. Reduce heat and simmer uncovered for 10 minutes, stirring frequently. Add prawns and simmer, stirring, until they curl and turn pink. Stir in lime juice and serve with hot rice.

Eggs Foo Yong with Prawns
Shallow-fry, serves 4

- 250 g (8 oz) cooked prawns
- 6 eggs
- ½ teaspoon salt
- ¼ teaspoon ground black pepper
- 6 spring onions, finely chopped
- peanut oil for frying
- 2 tablespoons chopped coriander leaves for garnish

Sauce
- 1 tablespoon light soy sauce
- 4 tablespoons dry sherry
- 2 tablespoons rice vinegar or white wine vinegar
- 2 tablespoons white sugar
- 1 tablespoon cornflour
- 1 tablespoon shredded red ginger

Shell, devein and roughly chop prawns. Beat eggs with salt and pepper. Mix in prawns and spring onions.

Heat wok, add 2 teaspoons oil and swirl to coat centre. Pour in 2 tablespoons egg mixture. When browned on underside, turn and cook other side. Transfer to a plate and keep warm. Repeat until remaining mixture is used up.

Wipe out wok with kitchen paper. Combine soy sauce, sherry, vinegar, sugar and ¾ cup water in wok and stir over medium heat until sugar dissolves. Bring to boil. Blend cornflour with 2 tablespoons cold water, stir into sauce and cook, stirring constantly, until thickened. Add red ginger and mix through.

Serve with sauce and a sprinkling of coriander leaves.

If you think squid needs tenderising, marinate in bicarbonate of soda (½ teaspoon dissolved in 2 tablespoons water) for 3 hours. Rinse and continue with recipe.

SQUID WITH SNOW PEAS
Stir-fry, serves 4

- *375 g (12 oz) cleaned squid tubes*
- *125 g snow peas or sugar snap peas*
- *2 tablespoons peanut oil*
- *2 fresh red chillies, seeded and finely sliced*
- *½ teaspoon finely grated fresh ginger*
- *½ cup chicken stock*
- *1 teaspoon light soy sauce*
- *1 tablespoon oyster sauce*
- *2 teaspoons cornflour*

Wash squid. Slice open and score cleaned inner surface with parallel cuts 6 mm (¼ in) apart, holding knife at an angle of 45 degrees. Besides being decorative, this exposes more surface area and speeds cooking. Cut into bite-size pieces. String snow peas, wash and dry.

Heat 1 tablespoon oil in wok, add chillies, ginger and squid pieces. Stir-fry, tossing over high heat for 2 minutes or until squid turns opaque and curls—be careful not to overcook or it will be tough. Remove from wok and put aside. Heat remaining oil in wok and toss peas over high heat for a few seconds. Stir in stock, soy and oyster sauces and bring to boil. Blend cornflour with 2 tablespoons cold water and stir into sauce. Cook until thickened. Toss squid in sauce and serve immediately with rice.

Most wok enthusiasts have more than one of these utensils, and this is a recipe where you can use two woks for best results.

QUICK BOILED SIZZLING FISH
Boil/fry, serves 4

- 1 whole white fish, about 1 kg (2 lb)
- salt
- 1 onion, peeled and sliced
- few celery tops
- 8 slices fresh ginger
- 20 whole black peppercorns
- 1 tablespoon chicken stock powder
- 3 tablespoons peanut oil
- ½ cup finely diced fat bacon
- 1 tablespoon dark soy sauce
- 2 teaspoons oriental sesame oil
- spring onions for garnish

Buy fish cleaned and scaled. Scrub cavity with damp paper towel dipped in coarse salt to remove all traces of blood. Trim spines with sharp scissors.

Three-quarter fill wok with water and add onion, celery, ginger, peppercorns and chicken stock powder. Bring to boil and simmer 6 to 8 minutes so liquid develops flavour. Gently slide fish into the water and return to boil. Lower heat and poach gently for 8 minutes or until flesh is opaque when tested.

Lift out on wire spoon or two large fish slices, let excess liquid drain for a few seconds, and carefully place fish on a large platter.

While fish is cooking, heat oil in another wok and fry bacon until crisp, stirring. Mix soy sauce and sesame oil and pour over fish, then pour the sizzling hot oil and fried bacon over and serve at once.

Note Don't waste the stock in which the fish was cooked. Strain and cook some thin slices of winter melon or other Chinese vegetable in it for a few minutes and serve as soup.

One of the nicest ways of enjoying these ever-more-expensive molluscs, giving them the importance they deserve by cooking and serving them in their pretty shells.

STEAMED SCALLOPS
Steam, serves 4

- *12 scallops on the half shell*
- *1 tablespoon dry sherry*
- *2 teaspoons light soy*
- *1 teaspoon oyster sauce*
- *1 teaspoon ginger juice*
- *1 spring onion, finely sliced*

Remove any dark veins from scallops but leave bright roe. In a small bowl combine sherry, soy, oyster sauce and ginger juice (grate fresh ginger and squeeze out the juice). Spoon a scant teaspoonful of mixture over each scallop.

Put 3 cups water on to boil in a wok. Place scallops in steamer, scatter a few slices of spring onion on each and steam over boiling water for 4 or 5 minutes. Serve at once.

These scallops won't do much to assuage hunger, but make an impressive first course or appetiser, either on their own or arranged (in their shells) on a bed of Braised Lettuce (see p. 1).

One of the advantages of wok cooking is that, even when deep-frying, not much oil is needed because of the shape of the utensil.

SPICY FRIED FISH
Deep-fry, serves 4

- 8 dried shiitake (Chinese) mushrooms
- 750 g (1½ lb) fish fillets
- ½ cup cornflour
- ½ teaspoon salt
- ½ teaspoon five spice powder
- peanut oil for frying

SAUCE
- 1 tablespoon peanut oil
- 3 spring onions, sliced
- 1 clove garlic, finely chopped
- 2 tablespoons light soy sauce
- ½ teaspoon five spice powder
- 1 tablespoon sugar
- 1 scant teaspoon chilli bean sauce
- 2 teaspoons cornflour
- spring onion curls (see Note p. 19)

Soak mushrooms in hot water for 30 minutes. Squeeze excess water from mushrooms (reserve soaking water), discard stems and cut caps into halves or quarters. Slice fish into strips and dip in cornflour mixed with salt and five spice powder. Heat ½ cup oil in wok until a haze rises from surface. Add half the fish at a time and deep-fry for 2 minutes. Drain on absorbent paper and transfer to serving dish. Keep warm. Discard frying oil.

Wipe out wok with kitchen paper. Heat 1 tablespoon oil and stir-fry mushrooms, spring onions and garlic. Stir in soy sauce, five spice powder, sugar, chilli bean sauce and 1 cup of the mushroom soaking liquid. Simmer for 10 minutes. Add cornflour blended with 1 tablespoon water and bring to boil, stirring. Pour over fish. Garnish with spring onions and serve with hot white rice.

LOBSTER WITH GINGER
Fry/braise, serves 2

- *2 green lobster tails*
- *1 egg white, slightly beaten*
- *1 tablespoon cornflour*
- *3 cups peanut oil*
- *2 tablespoons finely shredded fresh ginger*
- *½ cup spring onions cut into 5 cm (2 in) pieces*
- *1 cup hot chicken stock*
- *3 teaspoons cornflour*

Chop lobster tails into pieces, coat with egg white, cornflour and 1 tablespoon peanut oil. Chill 30 minutes. Heat oil (saving 1 tablespoon) and deep-fry lobster until shell turns red and meat becomes white. Pour lobster and oil into a wire colander over a heat-proof bowl.

Return wok to heat with remaining oil, stir-fry ginger and spring onion for 10 seconds, return lobster. Add stock, cover and steam on high heat for 2 minutes. Stir in cornflour mixed with 1 tablespoon cold water until sauce boils and thickens. Serve at once.

FRIED FISH WITH CRAB SAUCE
Deep-fry, serves 4

- *750 g (1½ lb) white fish fillets*
- *½ teaspoon finely grated fresh ginger*
- *1 clove garlic, crushed*
- *salt to taste*
- *cornflour for coating fish*
- *peanut oil for deep-frying*

CRAB SAUCE
- *2 tablespoons peanut oil*
- *4 spring onions, chopped, including green*
- *1 teaspoon finely grated ginger*
- *1 cup chicken stock*
- *185 g (6 oz) crab meat*
- *pinch of sugar and salt to taste*
- *3 teaspoons cornflour*

Remove skin from fish, wash and dry with paper towels. Rub fish with ginger, garlic and salt. Cut into bite-size pieces and toss in cornflour. Heat oil in wok and quickly fry fish over medium heat, a few pieces at a time, for about 1 minute. Drain on paper towels, transfer to serving dish and keep warm.

Discard oil and wipe over wok. Heat 2 tablespoons peanut oil and fry spring onions and ginger for a few seconds over low heat, stirring constantly. Add stock, cover and simmer for 3 to 4 minutes. Add crab meat, heat for 1 minute. Adjust seasoning with sugar and salt. Blend cornflour with 2 tablespoons cold water and stir into sauce until it boils and thickens. Spoon sauce over fish and serve immediately.

STIR-FRIED PRAWNS WITH VEGETABLES
Stir-fry, serves 4

- *2 tablespoons small dried wood fungus or 1 large piece*
- *500 g (1 lb) small raw prawns*
- *250 g (8 oz) fresh bean sprouts*
- *125 g (4 oz) snow peas or sugar snap peas*
- *2 tablespoons peanut oil*
- *1 clove garlic, crushed*
- *1 teaspoon finely grated fresh ginger*
- *2 teaspoons cornflour*
- *1 teaspoon sugar*
- *1 tablespoon light soy sauce*
- *1 tablespoon dry sherry*
- *1 teaspoon oriental sesame oil*

Soak wood fungus in hot water for 10 minutes. It will swell to many times its size. Trim off gritty bits and cut in bite-size pieces. Shell prawns and remove sandy tract. Wash bean sprouts and drain, pinching off straggly ends. String snow peas.

Heat 1 tablespoon oil in wok. Add garlic and ginger and stir for 10 seconds, add bean sprouts and toss for 30 seconds—sprouts should be crisp. Remove from wok. Heat remaining oil and stir-fry prawns just until pink. Add snow peas and stir-fry 1 minute. Return bean sprouts to wok with wood fungus and heat through. Push food to side. Mix cornflour with ¼ cup water, sugar, soy sauce, sherry and sesame oil. Pour into wok and cook, stirring, until it thickens. Lightly toss ingredients in sauce and serve immediately with rice or noodles.

PRAWNS WITH CHILLI
Stir-fry, serves 4

- *750 g (1½ lb) raw prawns*
  - *2 fresh red chillies*
  - *1 fresh green chilli*
    - *1 clove garlic*
  - *1 tablespoon sugar*
- *2 teaspoons finely grated fresh ginger*
  - *2 tablespoons light soy sauce*
  - *2 tablespoons dry sherry*
  - *3 tablespoons peanut oil*
    - *3 spring onions, sliced*

Shell and devein prawns, then rinse and dry on paper towels. Seed chillies and slice finely. Crush garlic with a teaspoon of the sugar and mix with chillies and ginger. Stir remaining sugar with soy sauce and sherry, until sugar dissolves.

Heat oil in wok and stir-fry prawns until colour changes. Remove to a plate. In remaining oil fry chillies, garlic and ginger, stirring, until garlic is golden. Stir in sauce mixture. When hot add prawns and stir until heated through. Sprinkle with spring onion and serve at once with hot rice or noodles.

Note   Always wear gloves when handling chillies.

Various methods of cooking are used in this dish: the fish is shallow-fried, vegetables stir-fried, then liquid is added and the wok covered so they are briefly braised. The whole operation should still take only a short time.

FISH AND VEGETABLE COMBINATION
Serves 4 to 6

- 750 g (1½ lb) fish steaks (tuna, jewfish or other firm fish)
- salt
- 2 medium onions
- 1 red capsicum
- 125 g (4 oz) long (snake) beans
- 1 tablespoon hoi sin sauce
- 1 tablespoon light soy sauce
- 4 tablespoons peanut oil
- 2 cloves garlic, finely chopped
- 1½ teaspoons finely grated fresh ginger

Cut fish into serving pieces, discarding bones. Sprinkle with salt and set aside. Peel onions. Cut in eighths lengthwise, then cut each section across and separate into layers. Cut capsicum in strips and then into bite-size lengths. Cut beans into similar lengths. Keep each vegetable separate as cooking times vary. Combine hoi sin sauce with soy sauce and ½ cup water.

Heat peanut oil in wok, wipe fish with paper towels to remove excess moisture and fry over high heat, turning, so pieces are browned on both sides. Drain fish on paper towels and pour off all but one tablespoon of oil from wok. Stir-fry onions and capsicum on high heat for 1 minute, remove to a plate. Add ginger, garlic and beans and fry for 1 minute. Add sauce mixture, cover and simmer until beans are tender, about 3 minutes. Return fish, capsicum and onion to wok, simmer for a further minute to heat through. Serve with hot white rice.

CHILLI SQUID
Deep-fry, serves 4 to 6

- 750 g (1½ lb) cleaned squid
  - ½ teaspoon salt
    - 1 egg white
- 1 tablespoon cornflour
- 1 tablespoon peanut oil
- 1 medium-size red chilli
- 1 medium-size green chilli
  - 1 clove garlic
  - 6 spring onions
  - 1 teaspoon sugar
  - 1 teaspoon chilli oil
  - 2 teaspoons cornflour
  - peanut oil for frying
- 125 g (4 oz) snow peas or sugar snap peas

Slit squid with a sharp knife and score cleaned inner surface with parallel cuts 6 mm (¼ in) apart to make a pattern of small diamonds. Cut into pieces 5 cm (2 in) square. Mix squid with salt, egg white, cornflour and peanut oil. Cover and chill for at least 30 minutes.

Seed chillies and cut into thin slices. Chop garlic finely and cut spring onions diagonally into bite-size lengths. Mix sugar, chilli oil and salt to taste into ½ cup water. Blend cornflour with 2 tablespoons cold water.

Heat 1½ cups peanut oil in wok and when hot add half the squid and fry on high heat about 1 minute, just until squid curls. Scoop from wok at once with a large perforated spoon. Repeat with remaining squid. Pour oil into a heatproof bowl. It may be strained and used again. Return wok to heat with just a film of oil and stir-fry snow peas for 1 minute. Add garlic, chillies and spring onions and stir-fry over high heat for 1 minute.

Add sugar and chilli oil mixture and as soon as it boils stir in cornflour mixture until it thickens. Return drained squid and heat through—do not boil. Garnish with a chilli flower and serve with steamed rice.

Fish with Peanut Sauce
Deep-fry, serves 4

- *750 g (1½ lb) large fish steaks*
- *lemon juice*
- *salt and pepper*
- *cornflour*
- *peanut oil for frying*
- *2 tablespoons light soy sauce*
- *2 tablespoons peanut butter*
- *½ cup canned coconut milk*
- *1 tablespoon malt vinegar*
- *1 teaspoon sugar*
- *1 tablespoon chopped fresh coriander leaves*

Cut fish into serving pieces. Wash and dry thoroughly with paper towels. Rub surface with lemon juice and season with salt and pepper. Dust lightly with cornflour, shaking off excess.

Heat sufficient oil in wok to fry fish. Fry in batches, turning to brown both sides. Drain on paper towels. Pour off all but 1 tablespoon of oil. Stir soy sauce, peanut butter, coconut milk, vinegar and sugar in wok until simmering. Return fish to wok, spoon sauce over and simmer gently until heated through. Sprinkle with coriander and serve with hot rice.

STEAMED FISH WITH ALMONDS
Steam, serves 4

- *1 kg (2 lb) whole fish such as snapper, ocean perch or similar firm white fish*
- *salt*
- *1 teaspoon finely grated fresh ginger*
- *1 tablespoon light soy sauce*
- *1 tablespoon fine shreds of ginger*
- *¼ cup peanut oil*
- *¼ cup flaked almonds*
- *1 tablespoon soy sauce*
- *1 teaspoon oriental sesame oil*
- *3 spring onions, thinly sliced*

Have fish cleaned and scaled, leaving head and tail intact. Rub cavity with paper towels dipped in coarse salt and clean thoroughly. Rinse well. Trim fins and sharp spines with kitchen scissors. Rub fish inside and out with a mixture of ginger and soy sauce. Scatter with ginger shreds and half the spring onions.

Place fish on a heatproof dish in a steamer. Boil 3 cups water in wok, cover steamer and steam fish for 10 to 12 minutes, or until cooked. Test at thickest part—flesh should be opaque. Lift dish from steamer, cover with foil and keep warm. Discard water and dry wok.

Heat peanut oil in wok and fry almonds over medium

heat until pale golden. Lift out with slotted spoon and drain on paper towel. Pour 2 tablespoons of hot oil over fish. Mix soy sauce and sesame oil and also pour over fish. Garnish with almonds and sliced spring onions and serve at once.

SPICY FISH IN COCONUT MILK
Simmer, serves 4 to 6

- *750 g (1½ lb) firm dark fish steaks such as tuna, mackerel, or bonito*
- *salt*
- *2 tablespoons lime or lemon juice*
- *2 onions, chopped*
- *3 cloves garlic, crushed*
- *2 teaspoons finely chopped fresh ginger*
- *1 stalk lemon grass or 2 strips lemon rind*
- *1 teaspoon ground turmeric*
- *½ teaspoon dried shrimp paste*
- *1 teaspoon chopped fresh chilli or sambal ulek*
- *1½ cups canned coconut milk*
- *1 tablespoon tamarind purée*
- *about 20 leaves fresh basil*

Wash and dry fish, sprinkle with salt and lime or lemon juice. Place onions, garlic, ginger, lemon grass, turmeric, shrimp paste and sambal ulek in electric blender and blend to a purée. Pour into wok and stir in ½ cup coconut milk thinned with 1 cup water. Heat until simmering and cook, uncovered, until liquid is reduced and thickened.

Dissolve tamarind in ¼ cup hot water. Add to wok with fish and simmer until fish is cooked. Add remaining coconut milk and basil leaves and heat through, stirring gently, so that it does not curdle. Do not allow to boil. Serve with hot rice.

CHICKEN

With the accent on speedy cooking, for most of these recipes you can do no better than buy chicken already filleted and free of skin. In some recipes, however, flavour will be lost if chicken is not cut the Asian way—not just jointed, but cut with a cleaver through the bones. The marrow and juices from the bones add to the taste and the pieces are small enough for all the flavours to penetrate. The bite-size morsels are easily managed with chopsticks and bones are politely discarded on the bone plate which is part of the Chinese place setting. (Provide saucers if you don't have bone plates.)

Use quick, decisive movements for chopping through bones and make sure the cleaver is sharp and has a suitably thick blade— a fine knife would be ruined.

Take care not to overcook chicken, especially breast fillets. Diced chicken will be done in a minute or less over a high gas flame; over an electric hotplate it will take a little longer, but watch carefully—it is cooked as soon as it turns white.

CHICKEN WITH CORN AND CASHEWS
Steam/fry, serves 6

- 1.5 kg (3 lb) assorted chicken pieces
- 1 teaspoon salt or to taste
- ½ teaspoon five spice powder
- ½ cup peanut oil
- 1 cup raw cashews
- 2 cloves garlic, crushed
- 2 teaspoons finely grated fresh ginger
- ½ cup chicken stock
- 1 tablespoon light soy sauce
- 1 teaspoon sugar
- 3 teaspoons cornflour
- 1 x 425 g (15 oz) can baby corn cobs, drained

Chop chicken into bite-size pieces, wipe over with paper towel to remove any fragments of bone. Rub chicken with salt and five spice powder. Place in heatproof dish on steaming rack or trivet in wok with water to just below rack. Cover and steam 15 minutes, or until cooked. (Reserve any liquid that collects in dish and add to stock.)

Dry wok thoroughly. Add peanut oil and heat. Fry cashews over medium heat, stirring constantly, until golden brown. Remove with slotted spoon and drain on paper towels. Pour off all but 1 tablespoon oil from wok. Lower heat and fry garlic and ginger, stirring constantly, for a few seconds until they begin to colour. Add chicken stock, soy sauce and sugar. Blend cornflour with 1 tablespoon cold water. Bring mixture in wok to a brisk boil, stir in cornflour until sauce thickens, add corn and return to boil. Pour over chicken, scatter cashews over and serve with rice.

Beautifully simple, but what flavour!

STEAMED CHICKEN, CHINESE STYLE
Steam, serves 4

- *750 g (1½ lb) assorted chicken pieces
or half a 1.5 kg (3 lb) roasting chicken*
  - *1 tablespoon soy sauce*
  - *2 teaspoons dry sherry*
  - *2 teaspoons cornflour*
- *1 teaspoon fresh ginger, finely chopped*
  - *½ teaspoon sugar*
  - *½ teaspoon oriental sesame oil*
- *green vegetable such as broccoli, snow peas
or sugar snap peas*

On a wooden chopping board and using a sharp cleaver, chop chicken into bite-size pieces. If using half chicken, separate leg and wing from body before chopping through. Wipe with damp paper towel to remove bone fragments. Combine chicken with all other ingredients except vegetables and transfer to a heatproof plate.

Place plate on a bamboo steamer or trivet in wok with water to just below rack. Cover and bring quickly to boil. Steam on high heat for 15 minutes. Prepare vegetables, dividing broccoli into sprigs or removing strings from peas. Five minutes before end of cooking time arrange vegetables around chicken, replace cover and finish steaming. Serve hot with steamed rice.

BRAISED CHICKEN WITH VEGETABLES
Braise, serves 4 to 6

- *750 g (1½ lb) chicken thigh or breast fillets*
- *salt to taste*
- *1 teaspoon five spice powder*
- *1 red capsicum*
- *6 spring onions*
- *2 tablespoons peanut oil*
- *1 clove garlic, finely chopped*
- *1 teaspoon finely chopped fresh ginger*
- *1 tablespoon oyster sauce*
- *2 tablespoons dry sherry*
- *1 x 425 g (15 oz) can straw mushrooms or oyster mushrooms*
- *1 tablespoon cornflour*

Cut chicken into bite-size pieces, sprinkle with salt and five spice powder and set aside. Cut capsicum into squares. Leave 1 spring onion for garnish (see Note) and cut the rest into bite-size lengths, about 5 cm (2 in).

Heat wok, add peanut oil and stir-fry chicken in two batches, tossing over high heat until golden. Transfer to plate. Fry garlic, ginger, capsicum and spring onions, stirring constantly, for 1 minute. Add oyster sauce, sherry, mushrooms and their liquid. Bring to boil, return chicken to wok, cover and simmer for 5 minutes. Mix cornflour with 2 tablespoons cold water and stir into sauce until it boils and thickens. Serve hot garnished with spring onion curls and accompanied by rice.

Note Before starting to cook, cut spring onion (including green leaves) into 10 cm (4 in) lengths and fringe both ends with a sharp knife or pin. Place in a bowl of iced water and ends will curl in a few minutes. Set aside for garnish.

If you are able to obtain different varieties of fresh mushrooms, such as shiitake or oyster (abalone) mushrooms, combine them with cultivated mushrooms.

BRAISED CHICKEN WITH FRESH MUSHROOMS
Braise, serves 4

- *500 g (1 lb) fresh mushrooms*
- *500 g (1 lb) chicken thigh fillets*
- *3 tablespoons peanut oil*
- *1 teaspoon finely chopped fresh ginger*
- *1 teaspoon finely chopped garlic*
- *2 tablespoons dark soy sauce*
- *2 teaspoons chilli sauce*
- *1 teaspoon oriental sesame oil*

Wipe mushrooms with damp paper towel. Don't wash, as they absorb water. Trim stems and, if mushrooms are large, cut into pieces. Cut chicken into bite-size pieces.

Heat peanut oil in wok and fry ginger and garlic, stirring, until golden. Add chicken and stir-fry for 2 minutes over high heat. Stir in ½ cup water, soy sauce, chilli sauce and mushrooms. Cover and simmer for 10 minutes. Raise heat and cook, uncovered, until most of the liquid has evaporated. Add sesame oil, toss and serve with rice.

Children love this combination of flavours, and it makes great finger food for parties or picnics.

Braised Honey Chicken
Braise, serves 4 to 6

- 1 kg (2 lb) chicken wings
- 2 tablespoons peanut oil
- ½ cup dark soy sauce
- 2 tablespoons honey
- 1 star anise (8 segments)
- 3 tablespoons dry sherry
- 1 small clove garlic, finely chopped
- 1 teaspoon finely chopped fresh ginger
- 2 spring onions
- 2 tablespoons toasted sesame seeds, optional

Divide chicken wings at joints and discard wing tips. Heat oil and brown chicken over high heat. Add remaining ingredients (except sesame seeds), stirring well to dissolve honey. Cover and simmer over gentle heat for 25 minutes or until chicken wings are tender. Stir towards end of cooking to ensure that honey does not burn. Serve at room temperature sprinkled with sesame seeds and garnished with spring onions.

Unlike stir-fries, braised dishes can be cooked in larger quantities. Serve with steamed jasmine rice as in Thailand.

CHICKEN WITH PEANUT SAUCE
Braise, serves 6 to 8

- 1.5 kg (3 lb) chicken thigh fillets
- 2 tablespoons peanut oil
- 2 tablespoons Red Curry Paste (see below)
- 2 teaspoons finely chopped garlic
- 2 teaspoons finely chopped fresh ginger
- 1 cup canned coconut milk
- 2 tablespoons crunchy peanut butter
- 1 rounded teaspoon palm or brown sugar
- 2 tablespoons fish sauce

Cut thigh fillets into 2 or 3 pieces. Heat oil and fry Red Curry Paste, garlic and ginger over low heat, stirring constantly, until mixture smells beautifully fragrant. Add chicken and fry, turning to coat with curry paste. Add coconut milk mixed with 1 cup water and when boiling stir in peanut butter, palm sugar and fish sauce. Simmer, uncovered, until flavours mellow and chicken is cooked. Serve with freshly cooked rice.

RED CURRY PASTE
- 6 to 8 fresh red chillies
- 2 small brown onions, chopped
- 1 teaspoon black peppercorns
- 2 teaspoons ground cummin
- 1 tablespoon ground coriander
- 2 tablespoons chopped fresh coriander, including root
- 1 teaspoon salt
- 1 stem lemon grass, finely sliced
  or 2 teaspoons chopped lemon rind
- 2 teaspoons chopped galangal in brine
- 1 tablespoon chopped garlic
- 2 teaspoons dried shrimp paste
- 1 teaspoon turmeric
- 2 teaspoons paprika (see Note)

Remove stems from chillies (if you want curry to be as hot as it is in Thailand, leave seeds in). Cut chillies into pieces, then place in electric blender with all other ingredients. Blend to a smooth paste, stopping frequently to push ingredients down with a spatula. You may need a little extra water, to assist with blending. Store in refrigerator in tightly sealed glass jar for a month or more.

Note While paprika is not used in Thailand, I have added it to give the requisite red colour without too many red chillies.

BRAISED CHICKEN WITH PLUM SAUCE
Braise, serves 4

- *half a roasting chicken, about 750 g (1½ lb)*
- *2 tablespoons peanut oil*
- *1 large clove garlic, finely chopped*
- *1 teaspoon finely chopped fresh ginger*
- *2 tablespoons dry sherry*
- *2 tablespoons plum sauce*
- *1 tablespoon light soy sauce*
- *2 teaspoons cornflour*
- *2 spring onions cut in short lengths*

Chop chicken into bite-size pieces and wipe with damp paper to remove any bone fragments. Heat wok, add oil and swirl. Add chicken pieces and stir-fry, tossing over high heat until browned. Lower heat, add garlic and ginger. Stir-fry for 1 minute then add sherry, plum and soy sauces and mix well to coat chicken. Cover and simmer 10 minutes or until tender. Mix cornflour with ¼ cup cold water and add to wok, stirring until sauce thickens. Mix in spring onions, stirring for 1 minute. Serve accompanied by hot white rice.

No, not that colonel, but one who spent his working life in India and enjoyed the household cook's version of a western pot roast.

THE COLONEL'S CHICKEN
Braise, serves 6

- 1.5 kg (3 lb) chicken or chicken pieces
- 2 cloves garlic, crushed
- salt to taste
- 1 teaspoon ground turmeric
- ½ teaspoon ground black pepper
- 4 tablespoons peanut oil
- 4 large onions, very thinly sliced
- 2 fresh red chillies, seeded and sliced
- 1 teaspoon garam masala

Joint chicken. Mix garlic, salt, turmeric and pepper and rub well into chicken. Leave for 30 minutes. Heat oil in wok and gently fry half the onions, stirring frequently, until brown. Remove onion from wok with slotted spoon and set aside.

Add a tablespoon more oil and stir-fry remaining onion and chillies until just starting to colour. Add chicken and fry over high heat until golden all over. Add ½ cup water, sprinkle with garam masala, cover and simmer, stirring occasionally, until tender, adding a little water if necessary. Uncover and cook quickly to reduce liquid. Serve hot, garnished with reserved fried onion and accompanied by rice or potatoes.

CHICKEN WITH SNOW PEAS
Stir-fry, serves 4

- *500 g (1 lb) chicken breast fillets*
  - *1 clove garlic, crushed*
- *½ teaspoon finely grated fresh ginger*
  - *1 tablespoon light soy sauce*
  - *1 tablespoon dry sherry*
- *125 g (4 oz) snow peas or sugar snap peas*
  - *2 tablespoons peanut oil*
  - *4 tablespoons chicken stock or water*
    - *1 teaspoon cornflour*

Cut chicken in very thin slices, mix with garlic, ginger, half the soy and half the sherry. String snow peas, drop into lightly salted boiling water. As soon as water returns to boil, drain and refresh peas in iced water to keep colour bright and texture crisp.

Heat oil in wok and stir-fry chicken until it turns white. Add remaining soy, sherry and stock or water; simmer for 2 minutes. Blend cornflour with 1 tablespoon cold water and stir in until sauce thickens. Add snow peas and toss gently to mix. Serve immediately with hot rice.

The red, white and green of this dish are pleasingly colourful.

STIR-FRIED CHICKEN AND CAPSICUMS
Stir-fry, serves 4

- *375 g (12 oz) chicken breast fillets*
- *½ teaspoon salt*
- *1 tablespoon egg white*
- *2 teaspoons cornflour*
- *3 tablespoons peanut oil*
- *1 red capsicum*
- *1 green capsicum*
- *1 teaspoon finely grated fresh ginger*
- *2 cloves garlic, crushed*
- *½ cup chicken stock*
- *1 tablespoon dry sherry*
- *2 tablespoons light soy sauce*
- *2 teaspoons cornflour*

Cut chicken into bite-size pieces. Add salt, egg white, cornflour and 1 tablespoon of oil and mix well. Cover and chill for about 30 minutes. Core capsicums and cut into even-size squares or strips, discarding seeds.

Heat wok, add 1 tablespoon oil and stir-fry capsicums over high heat for 1 minute. Remove. Add remaining oil and fry ginger and garlic for a few seconds; add chicken and stir-fry for 1 to 2 minutes over high heat.

Mix chicken stock, sherry, soy sauce and cornflour together, pour into wok and stir until it boils and thickens. Return capsicums to wok and heat through. Transfer to serving dish and serve with rice.

STIR-FRIED CHICKEN WITH OYSTER SAUCE
Stir-fry, serves 4

- 500 g (1 lb) chicken breast fillets
- 1 small clove garlic, crushed
- ½ teaspoon grated fresh ginger
- ½ teaspoon salt
- 6 large dried shiitake (Chinese) mushrooms
- 125 g (4 oz) snow peas or sugar snap peas
- 3 spring onions
- 2 tablespoons peanut oil
- 2 tablespoons dry sherry
- 1 tablespoon oyster sauce
- 2 teaspoons cornflour

Cut chicken into dice. Mix with garlic, ginger and salt and set aside. Soak mushrooms in a bowl of hot water for 30 minutes. String snow peas and cut spring onions into short lengths. Squeeze excess water from mushrooms (reserve liquid), trim and discard stems. Slice caps.

Heat 1 tablespoon oil in wok and stir-fry vegetables for 2 minutes. Push to one side. Add remaining oil, raise heat, add chicken and stir-fry until it changes colour (this will only take a very short time). Add ½ cup reserved mushroom liquid, sherry and oyster sauce. Stir well and bring to boil. Blend cornflour with 2 tablespoons cold water and stir into liquid until it boils and thickens. Serve immediately with hot white rice.

The inland province of Szechwan is renowned for its hot, spicy flavours. But the many dried chillies are only for those who enjoy picking them up and biting into them, the flavour doesn't make the whole dish pungent.

BRAISED SZECHWAN CHICKEN
Braise, serves 4 to 6

- 1.5 kg (3 lb) chicken
- 1 teaspoon Szechwan peppercorns
- 1 teaspoon five spice powder
- 1 teaspoon salt
- ⅓ cup cornflour
- ½ cup chicken stock
- 2 teaspoons sugar
- 1 tablespoon soy sauce
- 1 teaspoon oriental sesame oil
- 1 teaspoon rice vinegar
- 2 tablespoons dry sherry
- ½ cup peanut oil for frying
- 12 dried red chillies, seeded
- 2 cloves garlic, finely chopped
- 2 teaspoons finely chopped fresh ginger
- 4 spring onions, chopped in 5 cm (2 in) lengths

Cut chicken into serving pieces, chopping through bones with a cleaver. Wipe over with damp kitchen paper to remove any fragments of bone. Reserve back and neck for stock. Discard tail and excess fat from cavity.

Toast Szechwan peppercorns in a dry pan until fragrant, then crush to powder. Mix with five spice powder, salt and cornflour (reserving 1 teaspoon for thickening). Toss chicken pieces in mixture. Dust off excess. Combine stock, sugar, soy sauce, sesame oil, vinegar and sherry.

Heat oil in wok and when very hot add one-third of the chicken pieces. Fry on high heat, tossing chicken to brown all over. Drain on paper towel. Repeat with remaining chicken, allowing oil to get hot again between batches. Pour off all but 2 tablespoons oil. Add chillies, garlic and ginger and fry for about 1 minute till garlic and ginger are golden and chillies darken. Add spring onions and toss for a few seconds, then add stock mixture and bring to boil. Return chicken to wok, cover and simmer until chicken is tender, about 20 minutes.

Mix reserved cornflour with 1 tablespoon cold water. Stir into sauce until it boils and thickens. Serve with hot white rice.

CHICKEN AND WALNUTS
Deep-fry/Stir-fry, serves 4

- 500 g (1 lb) chicken fillets
- 1 tablespoon cornflour
- ½ teaspoon five spice powder
- salt to taste
- 250 g (8 oz) broccoli
- ⅓ cup peanut oil
- 1 cup peeled walnuts
- 1 teaspoon finely grated fresh ginger
- ½ teaspoon crushed garlic
- 1 tablespoon light soy sauce
- 1 teaspoon sugar

Cut chicken into 2 cm (¾ in) cubes. Sprinkle cornflour, five spice powder and salt over chicken and mix well. Divide broccoli into small sprigs and blanch in lightly salted boiling water for 30 seconds. Drain, reserving liquid.

Heat peanut oil in wok and fry chicken in batches just until colour changes, no more than 1 minute. Drain. Fry walnuts over medium heat, stirring gently so they cook evenly. When golden, remove with slotted spoon and drain on paper towels. Pour off all but 1 tablespoon of oil, and fry ginger and garlic for a few seconds. Add soy sauce and sugar mixed with ½ cup liquid from broccoli, and return chicken and broccoli to wok until heated through. Toss walnuts through and serve at once.

Some surprising textures here, the slippery straw mushrooms and crunchy almonds providing good contrast.

CHICKEN WITH ALMONDS AND STRAW MUSHROOMS
Stir-fry, serves 4 to 6

- 500 g (1 lb) chicken breast fillets
- 1 tablespoon egg white
- 3 teaspoons cornflour
- salt to taste
- 1 small mustard cabbage
- 430 g (15 oz) can straw mushrooms
- ½ cup peanut oil
- 1 cup slivered almonds
- 1 teaspoon grated ginger
- ½ teaspoon crushed garlic
- ½ cup chicken stock
- 2 teaspoons oyster sauce
- 1 tablespoon light soy sauce

Cut chicken into bite-size pieces. Mix with egg white, 2 teaspoons cornflour and salt, cover and chill at least 30 minutes.

Wash mustard cabbage, trim away tough outer ends of leaves and slice stems. Drain straw mushrooms and cut each mushroom in half lengthwise.

Heat oil and deep-fry almonds until golden. Remove with

slotted spoon and drain on paper towels. Add one-third of chicken pieces and deep-fry over high heat just until they change colour—about 1 minute. Lift out with a slotted spoon and drain on paper towel. Repeat with remaining chicken.

Pour off all but 2 tablespoons oil. Fry ginger and garlic on low heat for a few seconds. Add mustard cabbage and stir-fry for 1 minute or until colour intensifies. Add mushrooms and stir-fry over high heat for 1 minute. Add stock, oyster sauce and soy sauce. Mix 1 teaspoon of cornflour with 1 tablespoon cold water and add to wok, stirring until sauce thickens. Return chicken to wok and heat through. Turn off heat; stir in almonds and serve immediately with hot rice or noodles.

CHICKEN WITH SMOKED OYSTERS
Fry/Simmer, serves 3 to 4

- *375 g (12 oz) chicken thigh fillets*
- *½ teaspoon five spice powder*
- *salt to taste*
- *2 teaspoons cornflour*
- *peanut oil for frying*
- *½ cup chicken stock*
- *1 clove garlic, crushed*
- *1 x 100 g (3½ oz) can smoked oysters*

Cut chicken into small dice. Mix five spice powder, salt and cornflour. Toss chicken in this mixture to coat. Dust off excess.

Heat ⅓ cup oil in wok. Add garlic and chicken and deep-fry 2 to 3 minutes or until chicken starts to change colour. Push chicken to side of wok and add garlic stirring until it turns pale gold. Pour in stock. Mix cornflour with 2 tablespoons cold water. Add to wok and stir over medium heat until sauce boils and thickens. Add oysters and toss all ingredients together until heated through. Serve with hot rice.

If purchasing cutlets with the skin but no bone, this weight of chicken served with rice will be sufficient for 3 or 4 people because the sauce is so spicy; but if buying chicken on the bone, allow a thigh for each person.

SPICY TAMARIND CHICKEN
Braise, serves 3 to 4

- 375 g (12 oz) chicken thigh cutlets
- 2 tablespoons tamarind purée
- 2 tablespoons dark soy sauce
- 3 teaspoons ground coriander
- 2 teaspoons ground cummin
- 1 teaspoon chilli powder or to taste
- ½ teaspoon ground turmeric
- 2 teaspoons crushed garlic
- 2 teaspoons finely grated ginger
- ½ teaspoon shrimp paste
- ½ teaspoon salt
- 1½ tablespoons peanut oil
- 1 teaspoon palm sugar or brown sugar

Bone chicken if necessary, and use bones to make stock. Cut chicken into large pieces, leaving skin on. Thoroughly combine remaining ingredients except oil and palm sugar. Pour this mixture over chicken, rubbing in well. Cover and marinate at least 30 minutes, or refrigerate for longer.

Heat wok, pour in oil and fry chicken on medium high heat until colour changes, about 3 minutes. Add any remaining marinade, ¼ cup water and palm sugar, stir well, cover and cook for 5 minutes, ensuring palm sugar dissolves. Turn pieces over high heat until coated with sauce. Serve with rice and a vegetable dish with gravy.

Note   When chicken is cooked with skin, the fat content of the dish is much higher than when skinless fillets are used. To get rid of fat let dish sit for a few minutes and spoon off oil which rises to top.

A Thai dish usually made with chicken on the bone, chopped through in the Asian manner into bite-size pieces. For even quicker preparation and cooking, use convenient fillets.

CHICKEN WITH GINGER
Stir-fry, serves 4

- 500 g (1 lb) chicken thigh fillets or half a roasting chicken
- 3 cloves garlic, crushed
- 2 tablespoons peanut oil
- 2 tablespoons fish sauce
- 1 tablespoon vinegar
- 1 teaspoon dark soy sauce
- 2 teaspoons palm sugar
- 2 tablespoons finely shredded fresh ginger
- 1 teaspoon cornflour
- few sprigs fresh mint leaves torn in pieces

Cut chicken into bite-size pieces. Heat oil and fry garlic for 10 seconds, then add chicken and stir-fry until all chicken is golden. Add fish sauce, vinegar, soy sauce, palm sugar, ginger and ¼ cup water, cover and simmer for 3 minutes if using chicken fillets or, if chicken on the bone, until flesh near bone is no longer pink. Add cornflour blended with 1 tablespoon cold water and stir until thickened. Sprinkle with mint and serve with steamed rice.

EGGS IN SOY SAUCE
Simmer, serves 4 to 6

- *2 tablespoons peanut oil*
- *1 small onion, finely sliced*
- *1 fresh red chilli, seeded and sliced*
- *1 clove garlic, crushed*
- *1 teaspoon finely grated fresh ginger*
- *½ teaspoon dried shrimp paste*
- *1 large ripe tomato, peeled and diced*
- *1 tablespoon vinegar*
- *salt to taste*
- *1 tablespoon palm sugar or brown sugar*
- *3 tablespoons light soy sauce*
- *4 to 6 hard-boiled eggs*

Heat oil in wok and fry onion, chilli, garlic and ginger over gentle heat, stirring constantly until onion is soft and golden. Add shrimp paste and fry, mashing with back of spoon. Add tomato and cook, stirring, until tomato is very soft. Add vinegar, salt, sugar, soy sauce and ½ cup of water. Cover and simmer, stirring occasionally, until sauce is reduced and thick. Meanwhile shell eggs and cut into halves lengthways. Add to sauce in wok and simmer until heated through.

Meat

You can't cook a large slab of meat quickly, so sharpen up your knives and be prepared to slice meat thinner than for any western recipe. To make it easy to cut meat in paper-thin slices, partially freeze it first to make it firm.

Because meat is cooked for only 3 or 4 minutes, it has to be good quality fillet or rump steak and these are not exactly cheap— but you don't have to unbalance the budget. With forward planning you can use economy cuts such as round, blade or silverside. The cooking will be just as quick, but the meat first has to be marinated for some hours with a tenderising mixture which is the secret of many a Chinese restaurant.

Dissolve ½ teaspoon bicarbonate of soda in 3 tablespoons hot water, pour over 500 g (1 lb) finely sliced meat and mix well until all the water is absorbed. Cover and refrigerate for at least 2 hours, preferably longer, then proceed with the recipe. The meat will be very tender.

STIR-FRIED PORK WITH CASHEWS
Stir-fry, serves 4

- 375 g (12 oz) lean, tender pork
  - 1 medium onion
- 1 red or green capsicum (or half of each)
  - 3 tablespoons peanut oil
    - ½ cup raw cashews
  - 1 clove garlic, finely chopped
- ½ teaspoon finely chopped fresh ginger
  - 2 teaspoons light soy sauce
    - 2 tablespoons dry sherry
      - 1 teaspoon cornflour
- 1 spring onion, sliced diagonally into small pieces

Partially freeze pork to firm and cut in paper-thin slices. Peel onion, cut in quarters lengthwise and then in halves across. Separate layers. Cut capsicums to similar size and shape.

Heat oil and fry cashews until golden brown. Remove with slotted spoon and drain on paper towel. Add capsicum and onion and stir-fry on high heat for 1 minute. Remove to plate. In remaining oil stir-fry garlic and ginger for 30 seconds. Add pork and stir-fry until colour changes. Add soy sauce and sherry, cover and simmer for 2 minutes. Push pork to side of wok. Mix cornflour with 2 tablespoons cold water, add to wok and stir until sauce thickens. Return capsicum, onion and cashews, sprinkle with spring onion and serve at once.

Because everything is cut finely, this is really quick to cook. Serve with rice for a well balanced meal. Put rice on to cook before starting to stir-fry.

STIR-FRIED PORK AND THREE-COLOUR VEGETABLES
Stir-fry, serves 2

- *2 small carrots*
- *2 small zucchini*
- *1 stick celery*
- *250 g (8 oz) pork fillet*
- *1 tablespoon hoi sin sauce*
- *2 teaspoons cornflour*
- *1 tablespoon peanut oil*
- *1 clove garlic, crushed*
- *1 teaspoon finely chopped ginger*

Peel carrots and trim ends of zucchini. Cut all vegetables into fine julienne strips and set aside. Slice pork paper-thin. Combine hoi sin sauce with ½ cup water and cornflour.

Heat wok, add oil and stir-fry garlic and ginger over low heat for 30 seconds. Increase heat, add pork and stir fry, tossing, until browned. Add vegetables and stir-fry for about 2 minutes, until colour brightens and vegetables are tender but still crisp.

Push pork and vegetables to side of wok and pour hoi sin mixture into centre. Stir until sauce boils. Toss pork and vegetables through sauce.

The chilli bean sauce makes this a very zingy dish, but if your tastebuds are not attuned to chilli simply leave it out.

STIR-FRIED PORK WITH NOODLES
Stir-fry, serves 4

- 250 g (8 oz) lean, boneless pork
- 250 g (8 oz) egg noodles
- 3 tablespoons peanut oil
- 1 tablespoon dry sherry
- 2 tablespoons light soy sauce
- 1 red capsicum, sliced
- 2 cloves garlic, finely chopped
- 2 teaspoons finely chopped fresh ginger
- 2 teaspoons chilli bean sauce or to taste
- 2 fresh red chillies, seeded and finely chopped
- ½ cup sliced spring onions

Cut pork into paper-thin bite-size strips (this is easier if pork is frozen just long enough to make it firm). Unless using instant noodles (follow packet instructions), soak bundles of egg noodles in a bowl of warm water while bringing a pan of lightly salted water to boil. Drain noodles, drop into boiling water and cook for 2 minutes or until just tender. Drain in a colander, run cold water through and drain again. Drizzle 1 tablespoon peanut oil over and mix. Combine sherry and soy sauce.

Heat remaining oil in wok and stir-fry capsicum for 1 minute until colour intensifies. Remove to plate. Add garlic and ginger, and stir-fry until pale golden. Add pork and stir-fry until colour changes. Stir in bean sauce and cook over medium heat for 2 minutes. Add sherry mixture, capsicum and noodles and toss until heated through. Garnish with chillies and spring onions and serve hot.

STIR-FRIED BEEF IN OYSTER SAUCE
Stir-fry, serves 4

- *500 g (1 lb) tender lean beef*
- *2 tablespoons dark soy sauce*
- *2 tablespoons dry sherry*
- *2 teaspoons chilli sauce*
- *1 small green cucumber*
- *2 tablespoons peanut oil*
- *1 clove garlic, finely chopped*
- *2 teaspoons finely chopped fresh ginger*
- *2 tablespoons oyster sauce*
- *2 teaspoons cornflour*
- *4 spring onions cut in 2.5 cm (1 in) lengths*

Slice beef very thinly. Mix the soy sauce, sherry and chilli sauce and put half in bowl with the beef, mixing well. Leave to marinate. Cut cucumber in halves lengthwise and scoop out seeds. Cut each half across into thin slices.

Heat wok, add 1 tablespoon oil, and stir-fry cucumber for a few seconds. Remove with slotted spoon. Heat remaining oil, add garlic and ginger and fry for a few seconds. Add beef and stir-fry for 2 minutes or until colour changes. Add ½ cup water with oyster sauce and remaining marinade and bring to boil. Mix cornflour smoothly with 2 tablespoons cold water, add to wok, stirring constantly until liquid thickens. Stir in cucumber slices and spring onions and mix with beef. Serve immediately with hot rice or noodles.

A meat and fruit salad which makes a really tasty entrée or side dish.

THAI PORK MINCE WITH FRUIT
Stir-fry, serves 4

- 2 tablespoons peanut oil
- 1 tablespoon Pepper and Coriander Paste (see next page)
- 250 g (8 oz) minced pork
- 2 tablespoons fish sauce
- 1 tablespoon palm sugar
- 1 fresh red chilli, chopped
- 2 oranges
- half a small pineapple (see Note)
- ½ cup crushed roasted peanuts
- ½ cup crisp-fried shallots
- fresh mint leaves

Heat oil in wok and fry Pepper and Coriander Paste over low heat, stirring, until it smells fragrant. Add pork and stir-fry until all pork is browned. Add fish sauce, palm sugar, chilli and ½ cup water and stir well. Cook quickly until liquid is absorbed, stirring frequently. Turn off heat.

Peel oranges and cut in halves lengthways, then in crosswise slices. Cut away skin and 'eyes' from pineapple and cut lengthways in quarters. Discard core and cut into thin slices. Arrange fruit in a bowl, spooning pork mixture over.

Sprinkle with roasted peanuts and fried shallots and garnish with mint leaves. Serve at room temperature.

Note Try to buy a half-ripe pineapple, it is more suited to this recipe than a very ripe one.

PEPPER AND CORIANDER PASTE

A most useful mixture to have on hand when you wish to give your food a Thai flavour. Keeps for months in a clean, tightly covered glass jar in the refrigerator.
Makes about 1 cup

- *1 tablespoon finely chopped garlic*
- *2 teaspoons salt*
- *1 tablespoon whole black peppercorns*
- *1 cup firmly packed fresh coriander including roots and stems*
- *3 tablespoons lime or lemon juice*

With the flat of a knife, crush garlic with salt to a smooth paste. Roast peppercorns in a dry wok, stirring, for 2 minutes. Chop coriander finely and put everything into electric blender to purée, adding enough juice to facilitate blending. The paste may also be pounded in a mortar and pestle.

STIR-FRIED BEEF WITH CAPSICUMS
Stir-fry, serves 4

- 375 g (12 oz) tender lean beef
- 1 clove garlic, peeled
- salt to taste
- 1 teaspoon finely grated fresh ginger
- ½ teaspoon five spice powder
- 2 tablespoons soy sauce
- 1 green capsicum
- 1 red capsicum
- 250 g (8 oz) cauliflower florets
- 2 tablespoons peanut oil
- 2 teaspoons cornflour
- 1 teaspoon oriental sesame oil

Freeze beef until just firm and cut into paper-thin slices. Crush garlic with salt and add to beef with ginger, five spice powder and 2 teaspoons of soy sauce; mix well.

Discard seeds and membranes from capsicums and cut into wide strips, then into diamond shapes. Blanch cauliflower in boiling water for 1 minute. Drain.

Heat wok, add oil and when very hot, add beef and stir-fry until it changes colour. Add capsicums and toss for 1 minute. Add ½ cup water and remaining soy sauce. When liquid comes to boil, push meat and capsicums aside. Mix cornflour with 1 tablespoon of cold water and add to liquid in wok, stirring.

It will boil and thicken almost immediately. Add cauliflower, toss meat and vegetables through sauce. Sprinkle with sesame oil and serve immediately with rice.

Regulate the heat by choosing your chilli sauce carefully—there are many, from sweet and mildly hot to tongue-blistering!

SHREDDED CHILLI BEEF
Stir-fry, serves 4

- *500 g (1 lb) lean beef*
- *2 tablespoons dry sherry*
- *1 tablespoon dark soy sauce*
- *2 teaspoons chilli sauce*
- *2 teaspoons cornflour*
- *2 tablespoons peanut oil*
- *2 cloves garlic, finely chopped*
- *2 teaspoons finely chopped fresh ginger*
- *¼ cup finely chopped spring onions*
- *½ cup canned bamboo shoot, shredded*
- *½ cup zucchini, cut in julienne strips*
- *½ cup fresh red chillies, seeded and shredded*

Cut beef into very thin slices, then shred finely (easier if the meat is partially frozen). Combine sherry, soy and chilli sauces. Blend cornflour with ¼ cup cold water.

Heat oil in wok and stir-fry garlic, ginger and spring onions for 1 minute on medium heat, then raise heat and add shredded beef; stir-fry until colour changes. Add bamboo shoot, zucchini, chillies and stir-fry for 1 minute longer. Push beef to sides of wok, add sherry mixture and bring to boil. Add cornflour mixture and stir until liquid thickens. Toss beef through and serve immediately with hot white rice.

STIR-FRIED BEEF WITH MUSTARD CABBAGE
Stir-fry, serves 4

- 375 g (12 oz) lean steak
- 1 tablespoon dry sherry
- 1 clove garlic, crushed
- ½ teaspoon oriental sesame oil
- 1 teaspoon finely grated fresh ginger
- 2 tablespoons soy sauce
- 1 teaspoon sugar
- 1 teaspoon chilli bean sauce
- 2 tablespoons peanut oil
- 1 mustard cabbage, stalks cut across in thin slices
- 1 medium onion, cut lengthwise into eighths and layers separated
- 1 teaspoon cornflour

Slice steak thinly against grain and cut into bite-size pieces. Mix meat with sherry, garlic and sesame oil. In a separate small bowl combine ginger, soy sauce, sugar, chilli bean sauce and ¼ cup water, stirring until sugar is dissolved.

Heat 1 tablespoon oil and stir-fry vegetables over high heat for 2 minutes. Transfer to a dish. Heat remaining oil, add beef and fry over high heat until colour changes. Push beef to side of wok. Add liquid and bring to boil. Add cornflour mixed with 1 tablespoon cold water, stirring until thickened. Stir beef and vegetables through sauce. Serve with steamed rice.

If you like Thai food, here is a dish which will please your tastebuds.
Made with either of the pastes, it goes well with steamed rice.

BEEF WITH BROCCOLI
Braise, serves 4

- *375 g (12 oz) lean, tender steak*
- *250 g (8 oz) broccoli*
- *2 tablespoons peanut oil*
- *1 tablespoon Pepper and Coriander Paste (see p. 62)*
  or Red Curry Paste (see p. 43)
- *1 tablespoon fish sauce*
- *½ cup canned coconut milk*
- *2 kaffir lime leaves, fresh, frozen or dried*
- *2 teaspoons palm sugar or brown sugar*
- *2 red chillies finely sliced*
- *few fresh basil leaves*

Partially freeze beef until firm, and cut into thin, bite-size slices.
Divide broccoli into sprigs and blanch in boiling water for
1 minute, drain and refresh in iced water. Drain again.

Heat oil in wok and fry Pepper and Coriander or Red
Curry Paste over low heat, stirring, until fragrant. Add beef
and stir-fry until coated with paste. Add fish sauce and coconut
milk mixed with ½ cup water. Stir in kaffir lime leaves and
palm sugar and simmer for about 8 minutes. Serve sprinkled
with finely sliced chilli and fresh basil leaves.

A Thai influenced dish with a nice balance of hot, sweet and salty flavours.

Beef with Asparagus
Stir-fry, serves 4

- 375 g (12 oz) lean steak
- 250 g (8 oz) fresh asparagus
- 2 cloves garlic, peeled
- 1 tablespoon sugar
- 2 teaspoons green peppercorns in brine
- 1 tablespoon fish sauce
- 1 tablespoon Maggi Seasoning or oyster sauce
- 2 tablespoons peanut oil
- 1 teaspoon cornflour

Partially freeze steak and cut across grain into paper-thin slices. Wash asparagus well, snap off tough ends and cut in thin diagonal slices with a sharp knife, keeping tips whole. Crush garlic to a smooth paste with sugar, mash peppercorns and mix both with fish sauce, Maggi Seasoning or oyster sauce and 2 tablespoons water, stirring to dissolve sugar.

Heat 1 tablespoon oil in wok and fry steak over high heat until colour changes. Transfer to bowl. Wipe out wok, then heat remaining oil and stir-fry asparagus over high heat for 2 minutes. Add green peppercorn mixture, reduce heat, cover and cook for a few minutes or until asparagus is tender but still crisp. Push vegetables to side of wok. Mix cornflour with 1 tablespoon cold water and add to wok. Cook, stirring, until liquid boils and thickens. Return beef to pan, stir all ingredients gently together and cook just until heated through. Serve immediately with steamed rice.

Note Maggi Seasoning is a Swiss product I use instead of Thai Golden Mountain Sauce as it has similar flavour and no added monosodium glutamate.

MONGOLIAN LAMB
Stir-fry, serves 4

- 500 g (1 lb) lamb leg fillet
- 1 tablespoon dark soy sauce
- 1 teaspoon sugar
- ½ teaspoon salt
- 1 egg white, slightly beaten
- 3 teaspoons cornflour
- 4 tablespoons peanut oil
- 2 medium onions cut in wedges
- 3 cloves garlic, finely chopped
- 2 tablespoons hoi sin sauce
- 1 tablespoon refined bean sauce
- 1 teaspoon chilli bean sauce
- 2 tablespoons dry sherry

Place lamb fillet in freezer until firm enough to slice very thinly into bite-size pieces. Soak in cold water to cover for 30 minutes, pour off water and rinse again. (This helps eliminate any strong lamb flavour.) Press out excess water. Marinate meat in soy sauce, sugar, salt, egg white, cornflour and 1 tablespoon oil for 30 minutes.

Heat 1 tablespoon oil in wok and stir-fry onions for 1 minute. Remove to plate. Heat remaining 2 tablespoons oil and fry garlic for a few seconds. Add marinated lamb and fry on high heat, tossing constantly until colour changes. Stir in hoi sin, refined bean and chilli bean sauces mixed with ¼ cup water, boil for 2 minutes, stirring. Pour in sherry around side of wok, return onions and toss again to mix well. Serve with steamed rice.

Lamb is not usually associated with far-eastern cooking, but if the distinctive flavour is disguised somewhat by lots of chilli and garlic, it is quite acceptable to Asian tastebuds.

LAMB WITH CHILLI
Serves 4

- 500 g (1 lb) lamb fillets
- 1 teaspoon finely grated fresh ginger
- 4 cloves garlic, crushed
- 1½ tablespoons light soy sauce
- 1 tablespoon medium hot chilli sauce
- 1 tablespoon sherry
- 1 tablespoon oyster sauce
- 2 teaspoons sugar
- 3 tablespoons peanut oil
- half an iceberg lettuce
- 1 teaspoon oriental sesame oil

Cut lamb into thin slices and rub with ginger, garlic and 2 teaspoons of soy sauce. Combine chilli sauce, sherry, oyster sauce and sugar with 2 tablespoons water and remaining soy, stirring until sugar dissolves.

Heat wok, add 2 tablespoons peanut oil and when hot stir-fry lamb on high heat until it changes colour. Pour in combined sauce mixture, tossing until lamb is browned and coated. Transfer to plate. Cut lettuce in halves lengthways, then cut each half twice vertically and twice horizontally. Add remaining peanut oil to wok and toss lettuce until colour intensifies. Sprinkle with sesame oil, transfer to a serving plate and arrange lamb on top. Serve at once.

INDONESIAN TASTY MINCE
Serves 4

- 2 tablespoons peanut oil
- 1 onion, finely chopped
- 3 cloves garlic, peeled
- 1 teaspoon salt
- 1 teaspoon finely chopped fresh ginger
- 2 small red chillies, sliced
- 3 teaspoons ground coriander
- 2 teaspoons ground cummin
- 500 g (1 lb) lean minced steak
- ¼ teaspoon freshly ground black pepper
- ¼ cup chopped fresh mint
- ½ cup finely chopped spring onions

Heat oil and fry onion, garlic crushed with salt, ginger and chillies over low heat, stirring until soft. Add coriander and cummin, fry a few seconds longer, then brown steak, breaking it up with cooking spoon and turning it over and over so all meat is browned. Sprinkle with pepper. Cover and simmer until all liquid from meat is absorbed and meat is tender, about 10 minutes. Stir in mint and spring onions for last couple of minutes of cooking and serve with steamed rice and some vegetable accompaniments.

RICE AND NOODLES

OK, you knew there had to be a catch somewhere, and here it is. There is something a wok cannot do. I've been singing the praises of this wonderful utensil in which you can boil, braise, fry, simmer or stew. All true. The thing a wok cannot do is cook rice by the absorption method—that needs a pot with a well-fitting lid to hold the steam in. However, when it comes to fried rice and noodles, what else but a wok with its widely flaring sides can prevent bits and pieces ending up all over the cooktop. Go ahead and toss with abandon—the wok is ideal for frying and flavouring and adding diced meats to make a meal from cooked rice and noodles.

Rice is the mainstay of all Asian meals. Long grain rice needs slightly more water than short grain and both more than double in volume when cooked. Leftover rice keeps well in the refrigerator and is the base for many a tasty variation on fried rice which, incidentally, is served as a one-course meal, not accompanied by other dishes.

STEAMED RICE

- *2½ cups long grain rice*
- *3½ cups water*

Wash rice if necessary and drain in a colander. Put rice into a heavy saucepan with a well-fitting lid and add water. Bring quickly to boil, cover pan and turn heat very low. Cook for 15 minutes without lifting lid. Remove from heat and leave, still covered, for 10 minutes.

For fried rice, turn out immediately onto a tray to cool. Refrigerate overnight, and you will have firm, separate grains, the perfect starting point.

MIXED FRIED RICE
Stir-fry, serves 4

- *3 tablespoons peanut oil*
- *2 large leeks, finely sliced*
- *3 fresh chillies, seeded and sliced*
- *250 g (8 oz) roast pork or ham, sliced*
- *3 eggs*
- *salt and black pepper to taste*
- *4 cups cold cooked rice (see above)*
- *2 tablespoons light soy sauce*
- *2 tablespoons chopped coriander leaves*

Heat oil in wok and stir-fry leeks, chillies and pork or ham until leeks are soft and golden. Beat eggs, salt and pepper, pour into wok and cook, stirring over medium heat until set. Stir in rice and sprinkle with soy sauce. Toss until heated through. Sprinkle with coriander leaves and serve.

CHILLI FRIED RICE
Stir-fry, serves 4

- 3 tablespoons peanut oil
- 2 medium onions, finely chopped
- 2 fresh chillies, 1 red and 1 green, seeded and sliced finely
- 2 cloves garlic, finely chopped
- 250 g (8 oz) boneless pork or chicken, finely diced
- 250 g (8 oz) raw or cooked prawns, shelled and deveined
- 4 cups cooked rice (see p. 72)
- 2 eggs, beaten
- 1 tablespoon light soy sauce
- pepper to taste
- 2 tablespoons fish sauce
- 1 tablespoon hot chilli sauce
- 1 tablespoon fresh lime or lemon juice
- 1 teaspoon sugar
- ½ cup chopped spring onions, including green tops
- ½ cup chopped fresh coriander leaves

Heat wok, add oil and fry onions, chillies and garlic until soft, saving a few chilli slices for garnish. Add pork or chicken and stir-fry until cooked. Stir in prawns (roughly chopped if large) and cook until colour changes. Add rice and stir-fry until heated through.

Push rice mixture to side of wok and pour eggs, mixed with soy sauce and pepper into centre. Stir until eggs are set.

With wok chan (spatula), cut egg into small pieces. Mix fish and chilli sauces, lime juice and sugar and sprinkle over rice. Toss eggs and rice mixture together over high heat for 1 minute. Remove from heat, and toss spring onions and coriander leaves through rice. Garnish with chilli slices and serve immediately.

FRIED RICE WITH BARBECUED PORK
Stir-fry, serves 4

- *375 g (12 oz) Chinese barbecued pork*
- *1 x 250 g (8 oz) can water chestnuts*
- *2 tablespoons peanut oil*
- *1 clove garlic, crushed*
- *1 teaspoon finely chopped fresh ginger*
- *4 cups cold cooked rice (see p. 72)*
- *2 tablespoons soy sauce*
- *1 tablespoon dry sherry*
- *salt and pepper to taste*
- *½ cup finely sliced spring onions*

Buy a strip of pork with a little bit of fat on it. Separate fat from meat and cut each into small dice keeping separate. Drain water chestnuts and chop. Heat pork fat and oil in wok until fat melts. Add pork, fry until brown and remove with a slotted spoon. Stir-fry garlic and ginger over low heat for a few seconds without browning.

Add rice and cook over high heat, stirring and tossing constantly, until rice begins to colour. Sprinkle with soy sauce and sherry. Add pork, water chestnuts, spring onions and toss thoroughly through rice. Serve hot.

Lap cheong are the Chinese equivalent of salami, but with a unique flavour. They need to be steamed until soft before using.

SPRING ONION AND SAUSAGE FRIED RICE
Stir-fry, serves 4

- 4 Chinese dried sausages (lap cheong)
- 2 tablespoons peanut oil
- 2 cloves garlic, finely chopped
- 4 cups cold cooked rice (see p. 72)
- 2 tablespoons light soy sauce
- 6 spring onions, sliced

Steam lap cheong over boiling water for 10 minutes or until plump and fat is transparent. (This is easily done in wok, but rinse and dry wok well before adding oil for frying.) Cut lap cheong into thin diagonal slices.

Heat oil in wok, fry garlic for a few seconds, add sliced sausage and toss for 1 minute. Add rice and stir-fry until grains are separate and lightly coloured. Sprinkle with soy sauce and spring onions and toss to mix and heat through. Serve immediately.

Like most Asian dishes, this is a free-wheeling combination which you can tailor to your taste and availability of ingredients. You will find fresh Hokkien (thick yellow) noodles at Asian supermarkets or you can use dried egg noodles instead. This dish epitomises the flavours of Singapore and Malaysia, and is a meal in itself.

Fried Noodles
Stir-fry, serves 4

- 500 g fresh Hokkien mee or 375 g (12 oz) fine egg noodles
- 250 g (8 oz) firm bean curd
- 250 g (8 oz) small raw prawns
- 3 tablespoons peanut oil
- 1 onion, finely chopped
- 5 cloves garlic, finely chopped
- 2 teaspoons finely chopped fresh ginger
- 1 or more fresh red chillies, seeded and sliced
- 1 teaspoon dried shrimp paste
- 5 stalks Chinese celery, finely sliced
- 2 tablespoons light soy sauce
- ½ cup chopped garlic chives
- thinly sliced cucumber
- lime wedges

Rinse Hokkien noodles in hot water and drain. If using dried noodles, soak in warm water while bringing lightly salted water to boil in a large pan. Drain noodles, drop into boiling water and return to boil for 2 minutes. Noodles must be tender but still firm to bite. Drain immediately in a colander, rinsing with cold water to stop them cooking in their own heat. Drain again.

Cut bean curd into small dice. Shell and devein prawns. Heat oil in wok and fry onion, garlic and chilli until onion starts to turn golden. Stir in shrimp paste, crushing with back of spoon as it cooks. Add bean curd, prawns and celery, stir-fry until cooked. Add drained noodles and toss to heat. Add soy sauce to taste. Transfer to serving dish and sprinkle with garlic chives. Arrange cucumber slices and lime wedges around edge of dish. Serve with chilli sauce.

*A romantic name for thin, transparent noodles made from mung
bean starch. They have no flavour of their own, so do little to
mute this dish's fiery flavour.*

SPRING RAIN NOODLES WITH PORK
Stir-fry, serves 4

- 6 dried shiitake (Chinese) mushrooms
- 100 g (3½ oz) bean thread vermicelli
- 3 tablespoons peanut oil
- 4 spring onions, finely chopped
- 2 teaspoons finely chopped fresh ginger
- 1 teaspoon crushed garlic
- 250 g (8 oz) minced pork
- 1 tablespoon dry sherry
- 1 tablespoon light soy sauce
- 1 tablespoon hot chilli bean sauce
- 1 cup chicken stock
- 2 red chillies, seeded and sliced
- fresh coriander leaves for garnish

Soak mushrooms in hot water for 30 minutes then discard
stems and dice caps finely. Cover noodles with boiling water
and soak for 10 minutes or until soft and transparent. Drain
in colander then cut into manageable lengths.

Place wok over high heat. Pour in oil and when hot add
spring onions, ginger, garlic, pork and mushrooms. Fry until

pork is browned. Stir in sherry, soy and chilli bean sauces. Cook over medium heat for 1 minute. Add stock and when boiling add noodles and cook on low heat until all liquid has been absorbed. Sprinkle with sliced chilli and coriander leaves and serve immediately.

✳ RICE NOODLES IN SPICY SAUCE
Shallow-fry, serves 4

- *375 g (12 oz) rice vermicelli*
- *4 tablespoons Red Curry Paste (see p. 43)*
- *3 tablespoons peanut oil*
- *1 tablespoon fish sauce*
- *2 tablespoons salted black beans*
- *3 teaspoons brown sugar*
- *1 x 400 mL can coconut milk*
- *¼ cup tamarind liquid*
- *8 cubes fried bean curd*
- *1 cup roughly chopped garlic chives or spring onions*
- *4 hard-boiled eggs, quartered*
- *chilli slices and lime wedges*

Soak rice vermicelli in boiling water for 2 minutes, then drain in colander.

Heat peanut oil in wok and on low heat fry curry paste, stirring frequently, for about 5 minutes or until fragrant. Turn off heat. Stir in fish sauce, black beans and brown sugar and put half the mixture into a saucepan with coconut milk and an equal amount of water. Bring to simmering point and stir in tamarind and fried bean curd, sliced.

Reheat curry paste gently, add rice vermicelli and toss over medium heat, adding chives. For each serve, put some vermicelli into a large bowl, ladle some of the gravy over and garnish wtih hard-boiled eggs and chilli slices; offer lime wedges so that guests season their food 'to taste'.

Potato is not used as a filler or starch component here but deep-fried in tiny dice for texture and flavour.

RICE VERMICELLI WITH CHICKEN AND POTATO
Stir-fry, serves 4 to 6

- 375 g (12 oz) rice vermicelli
- 250 g (8 oz) chicken breast fillets
- 1 large raw potato, peeled and finely diced
- ¼ cup peanut oil
- 2 medium onions, finely sliced
- 2 large cloves garlic, finely chopped
- 2 tablespoons light soy sauce
- ¼ teaspoon ground black pepper
- 2 teaspoons sugar
- 1 tablespoon chilli sauce
- salt to taste
- ½ cup chopped spring onions

Soak rice vermicelli in hot water for 5 minutes then drain in colander. Cut chicken into bite-size pieces. Soak diced potato in cold water, drain and dry on paper towels. Heat wok. Pour oil into wok and when a haze rises from surface add diced potato and deep-fry over high heat for 2 minutes. Reduce heat to medium and continue cooking until golden brown and cooked through. Remove with a slotted spoon and set aside.

Pour off oil, leaving about 2 tablespoons. Add onions and garlic and fry for 2 minutes, stirring constantly, over medium heat. Add chicken, stir-fry until flesh turns white. Mix soy sauce, pepper, sugar and chilli sauce into ½ cup water, pour into wok and bring to boil. Add rice vermicelli, stir, cover and simmer for 3 minutes or until liquid is absorbed. Mix in potatoes, add salt to taste and serve immediately, sprinkle with spring onions.

No time to cook? With instant noodles and a wok, a meal in minutes is entirely achievable. Of course, it helps if your refrigerator yields cooked meats and fresh vegetables.

INSTANT NOODLE MEAL
Boil, serves 2

- *2 packets instant soup noodles*
- *2 stems Chinese cabbage or broccoli*
- *slices of cooked chicken, barbecued or roast pork or Chinese sausages*
- *2 teaspoons oriental sesame oil*
- *2 teaspoons ketjap manis (sweetened dark soy)*
- *sweet or hot chilli sauce to taste*

In a wok, bring 4 cups water to boil with soup flavouring from noodle packets. Cut vegetables into bite-size lengths and boil in liquid until tender but still crisp. Lift out on perforated spoon, drop in noodles and cook for 2 minutes or as specified on packet. Drain, saving liquid for soup. Return noodles to wok and toss with sliced meats, cooked vegetables, sesame oil, soy sauce and chilli sauce. Serve at once, with soup in separate bowls.

Stop at any food stall in Singapore and enjoy cha kway teow, rice noodles spiked with chillies and lots of small, tasty tidbits.

FRESH RICE NOODLES SINGAPORE STYLE
Serves 4 to 6

- 500 g (1 lb) fresh rice noodles (see Note)
- 3 tablespoons peanut oil
- 2 teaspoons finely chopped garlic
- 2 or 3 fresh chillies, finely chopped
- 100 g (3½ oz) chopped rump or fillet steak
- 2 rashers bacon or ham, chopped
- ½ cup chicken, chopped
- 1 cup cooked or frozen green peas
- 2 teaspoons chilli bean sauce
- 2 tablespoons oyster sauce
- ½ cup chopped spring onions
- 2 teaspoons oriental sesame oil

Cut rice noodles into thin strips and soak in lukewarm water until they separate easily. Drain well.

Heat wok, add oil and fry garlic and chillies, stirring, over medium heat until soft. Add steak, bacon and chicken and stir-fry until cooked. Add peas, chilli bean and oyster sauces and mix well then add noodles and toss gently to distribute sauces and flavourings. Sprinkle with spring onions and sesame oil and toss a few times to mix. Serve hot.

Note   You will find fresh rice noodles in Asian grocery stores called Sa Ho Fun. Use within a day or two. Do not refrigerate as this makes them hard and brittle.

A meal in one dish, made from bits and pieces you may find in the refrigerator.

SPICY NOODLE SOUP
Boil, serves 2

- 2 tablespoons peanut oil
- 1 small onion, finely sliced
- 2 tablespoons Pepper and Coriander Paste (see p. 62)
- 2 teaspoons finely grated fresh ginger
- 2 teaspoons ground coriander
- ½ teaspoon ground turmeric
- 4 cups hot chicken stock
- 1 cup canned coconut milk
- 2 kaffir lime leaves, fresh or frozen
- 125 g (4 oz) rice vermicelli
- 2 small boiled potatoes, sliced
- 2 hard-boiled eggs, sliced
- 1 cup cooked chicken, sliced
- 2 sprigs fresh coriander, roughly chopped
- crisp fried onions, optional (see Note)

Heat oil and over medium-low heat fry onion, Pepper and Coriander Paste, ginger, ground coriander and turmeric, stirring constantly, for about 5 minutes. Add chicken stock, coconut milk and lime leaves and bring to boil. Simmer about 10 minutes. Meanwhile, soak rice vermicelli in hot water for 10 minutes and drain. Drop into simmering soup and cook for 3 or 4 minutes. Serve in soup bowls topped with potatoes, eggs, chicken, coriander and crisp fried onions.

Note   Crisp fried onions are available at Asian shops.

Glossary

Most of these ingredients are found in Asian stores though many of them have made their way to supermarket shelves, health shops and the local greengrocer.

Bean curd Made from soy beans and high in protein, it is available fresh in various forms—soft, firm, fried. Soft bean curd has the consistency of junket or baked custard, and in Chinese shops is sold immersed in water, whereas Japanese brands are usually called silken tofu and are found in tetra packs. Firm bean curd (pressed bean curd) may be found in both yellow and white blocks. Much easier to cook because it does not break up when stirred. Fried bean curd comes in golden brown cubes with a creamy white, spongy interior. Usually sold in plastic bags. All types may be found in the refrigerator section of Asian stores. Fresh bean curd may be kept refrigerated for up to 3 days, but is best when absolutely fresh.

Bean curd is also sold dried and canned. While these have their uses, they should not be substituted for fresh.

Black beans Salted, fermented soy beans which come in cans or packets. Rinse away excess salt and use as recipe suggests.

Chilli bean sauce Sold in jars, it is very hot and should be used with discretion.

Chillies Fresh chillies should be handled with care as the volatile oils can cause much discomfort. Wear gloves especially when chopping. It is possible to buy fresh chopped chillies in jars which may be substituted, and also sambal ulek which is a mixture of fresh chillies and salt. Dried chillies should be soaked before using. Small chillies are hotter than large ones.

Coconut milk Canned coconut milk is readily available but some brands are very thick and rich, others extremely thin. The former should be diluted with water in equal parts, the latter used straight from the can. Usually the thicker ones are more expensive.

Coriander Coriander seeds and fresh coriander are totally different in flavour and usage. Dried ground coriander seeds are one of the main ingredients in curries. Fresh coriander herb is essential in Thai and Chinese cooking, among others.

Dried wood fungus Also known as 'cloud ear fungus' or 'wood ears' because of its convoluted shape. Resembles bits of black or grey paper in its dried state, but after soaking for 10 minutes or so it swells and turns into translucent brown cloud shapes. A flavourless ingredient, used for its texture.

Fish sauce A thin, salty sauce used in South-East Asian food.

Five spice powder A spice mixture much beloved in Chinese cooking. A combination of ground star anise, fennel, cinnamon, cloves and Szechwan pepper.

Galangal (Alpinia galanga) Also known as laos or lengkuas. An aromatic rhizome similar in size and appearance to ginger. May be bought fresh, frozen, dried, ground, or pickled in brine which is most convenient and keeps indefinitely in the refrigerator.

Garam masala Essential in Indian dishes, this is a spice blend worth making up. Roast separately until fragrant 2 tablespoons coriander seeds, 1 tablespoon cummin seeds, 2 teaspoons whole black peppercorns, 1 teaspoon cardamom seeds (remove from pods), 2 cinnamon sticks and 10 whole cloves. Grind as finely as possible and mix in half a nutmeg, finely grated. Store airtight.

GINGER Whenever ginger is mentioned in this book, it is fresh ginger root. Now sold at most greengrocers. Dried ground ginger is no substitute.

KAFFIR LIME LEAVES These are essential in Thai cooking and have a perfume unlike any other citrus leaves. They are sold fresh, frozen and dried.

KALONJI SEEDS (NIGELLA) These are sometimes called black cummin though not a member of the cummin family. The flavour is quite distinctive and there is no substitute. Mostly from Indian shops.

KETJAP MANIS *See* soy sauce.

LEMON GRASS An aromatic plant which grows easily in Australia. The part to use is the white or pale green portion of the stem which is tender enough to slice finely. Substitute 2 strips thinly peeled lemon rind for each stem of lemon grass.

MAGGI SEASONING A Swiss sauce similar in flavour to Thai Golden Mountain sauce but without added monosodium glutamate, and readily available in western supermarkets.

MUSHROOMS Dried Chinese or Japanese mushrooms are the shiitake variety. Their unique flavour cannot be duplicated by dried European mushrooms.

OYSTER SAUCE A thick, dark, oyster-flavoured sauce used in Chinese food.

PALM SUGAR Obtained from various tropical palms, it has a distinct flavour but may be substituted by brown sugar.

SAMBAL ULEK *See* **Chillies**.

SESAME OIL Whenever sesame oil is called for, use oriental sesame oil made from roasted sesame which is dark in colour and very aromatic. Light coloured sesame oil (usually sold in health food stores) will not impart the same flavour.

SHRIMP PASTE Made from dried shrimp, this is powerful stuff but used in tiny quantities makes a great difference in flavour and is a mainstay of South-East Asian cuisines. Sold in jars or blocks. Keeps indefinitely.

SOY SAUCE There are many types. For this book you need dark soy (thick, coloured with caramel); light soy (thin, saltier than dark); Indonesian sweetened soy (ketjap manis); and Japanese soy (shoyu). For best results, use the specified kind.

SZECHWAN PEPPER Small, reddish brown dried berries, they give special flavour and are not hot in the conventional sense, but give a numbing sensation on the tongue. Only the brown husks provide flavour, the small black seeds should be discarded, so buy the seeded variety. Roast over low heat to make them aromatic, and crush to powder.

TAMARIND Fruit of a tropical tree, tamarind imparts acidity to many dishes. It is sold dried, puréed or instant. The dried pulp has the truest flavour. To make tamarind liquid, soak 1 tablespoon dried tamarind in ½ cup hot water, dissolve pulp, strain. Or spoon the purée from a jar; or dissolve instant tamarind in hot water.

TURMERIC The rhizome is dried and ground to a yellow powder which has a distinctive flavour of its own and is used to flavour and colour rice and curries. A staple in commercial curry powders.

WOOD FUNGUS *See* **Dried wood fungus**.

INDEX